HEALING
with
RAW
FOODS

ALSO BY JENNY ROSS

THE ART OF RAW LIVING FOOD: Heal Yourself and the Planet with Eco-delicious Cuisine (with Doreen Virtue)

RAW BASICS: Incorporating Raw Living Foods into Your Diet Using Easy and Delicious Recipes

Please visit:

Hay House USA: www.hayhouse.com®
Hay House Australia: www.hayhouse.com.au
Hay House UK: www.hayhouse.co.uk
Hay House South Africa: www.hayhouse.co.za
Hay House India: www.hayhouse.co.in

HEALING
with
RAW
FOODS

YOUR GUIDE TO UNLOCKING VIBRANT
HEALTH THROUGH LIVING CUISINE

JENNY ROSS

HAY HOUSE, INC.
Carlsbad, California • New York City
London • Sydney • Johannesburg
Vancouver • Hong Kong • New Delhi

Published and distributed in the United States by: Hay House, Inc.: www.hayhouse.com® • *Published and distributed in Australia by:* Hay House Australia Pty. Ltd.: www.hayhouse.com.au • *Published and distributed in the United Kingdom by:* Hay House UK, Ltd.: www.hayhouse.co.uk • *Published and distributed in the Republic of South Africa by:* Hay House SA (Pty), Ltd.: www.hayhouse.co.za • *Distributed in Canada by:* Raincoast Books: www.raincoast.com • *Published in India by:* Hay House Publishers India: www.hayhouse.co.in

Cover design: Stonesong Creative • *Interior design:* Tricia Breidenthal
Interior photos: Fringe Photography

Cataloging-in-Publication Data is on file with the Library of Congress

Tradepaper ISBN: 978-1-4019-4038-6

10 9 8 7 6 5 4 3 2 1
1st edition, January 2015

Printed in the United States of America

To my children, Dylan James and Alysa Grace, whose world will be improved as living plant-based foods begin to heal those committed to a different reality for their health. My hope is that you both will continue to embrace these possibilities for your own vibrant health and will pass on these ideas to your children's children.

In loving memory of my grandparents, Charles Ross, Sr., John Peacock, and Gerry Peacock, who taught me the kind of life lessons that have helped me remain open to new possibilities. I am grateful for your lasting imprint on my life.

To my family for your continued support of this mission to help others find healing, even when it means long days at the restaurants! Your grace in my life is immeasurable.

CONTENTS

INTRODUCTION

"Natural forces within us are the true healers of disease."

— HIPPOCRATES

Imagine if you could invigorate your life just by changing what you eat! Would you alter your diet for a chance at sustained health and optimal longevity? How far would you go to attain your best body, best looks, clearest mind, and highest energy?

When I began my personal journey with raw foods a decade ago, my very health and well-being were at stake. For years I had suffered indigestion and low-level abdominal pain brought on by GERD (gastroesophageal reflux disease), IBS (irritable bowel syndrome), and an ulcer. One health problem is challenging enough, but when you face a series of issues, all diagnosed in your late teens, just getting through the day can be overwhelming. I was very depressed because of the constant pain. Something inside me screamed, "There must be a healthier, happier way to live, free from the disease plaguing my body!" I was looking for healing.

From that moment on I was committed to finding a new truth. I would do whatever necessary to accomplish that mission. Not surprisingly, allopathic or traditional medicine didn't lead me to the healing I was seeking. I came to recognize long after my health problems had been diagnosed that modern medicine isn't designed to address the body holistically, but rather treat symptoms as they occur. Even though what you eat is recognized as preventive in some cases, diet is rarely a sole treatment focus. That limitation, at least at the time, left me searching—and gratefully so—for alternatives. With my determination came the realization that my choice of food could not only heal my digestive tract but also support my *entire* body in optimal daily health.

Today, I'm proof that you can achieve just that by simply looking to the end of your fork. My personal path to healing led me into a lifestyle centering on the nonprocessed plant sources of a raw-foods diet. This nutrient-rich, high-energy approach to eating has yielded exponential results across my entire life. I've been living vibrantly for more than a decade, with a burgeoning raw-foods business, two healthy young children, and a supportive, loving husband. Together with our extended community of fellow food travelers, we've altered *what* and *how* we eat for the better. What do I mean by that? We've adopted a style of eating—"gourmet living cuisine"—that incorporates plant-based whole foods served either raw or prepared at 118°F or lower. Why that temperature? It is the threshold that lets us steer clear of any harmful substances created by high-temperature cooking while keeping enzyme and nutrient values intact.

By focusing on high-quality fruits, vegetables, nuts, seeds, and sprouted grains in their most natural state, I've experienced absolute freedom from my symptoms—the opposite of what you might expect from a seemingly *limited* diet. I healed my body from the inside out! Learning new ingredients and food preparation techniques while exploring the benefits of this lifestyle became a full-time adventure. I enjoyed my first mango . . . ate my first raw chocolate bar . . . and finished my first meal in five years pain-free! In time, I realized just how restrictive my life had been *before* these discoveries. Imagine my joy in learning something new that made me feel fantastic from head to toe!

I firmly believe that you, too, can reverse or prevent conditions that might rob you of your vitality and deprive you of your best chance to experience overall good health. The menu choices in *Healing with Raw Foods* are *anti-inflammatory* and *alkaline*, two terms that you'll become familiar with as you discover foods that can have a positive effect on your body, your mind, and even your spirit. I'm confident that the choices in this diet can help you realize your inner potential for living well, living holistically, and living fully to share your unique gifts with others.

Next in a Series

Healing with Raw Foods is the third cookbook in a series of books I've written to help you get the most from this exciting new cuisine. *The Art of Raw Living*, my first book, offered dietary fundamentals and easy recipes, along with simple steps for transitioning from a standard American diet (SAD) to living-foods fare. *Raw Basics*, my second book, merged favorite recipes from my California restaurants, 118 Degrees, with advice on successfully incorporating this diet into your lifestyle.

Although those books are great resources, you don't have to read them to enjoy or learn from this one. Everything you need to know about the foundational foods and dietary practices necessary to catapult your health to the next level, your highest truth, is contained in these pages. Think of this book as an important guide in your journey to wellness. Each chapter has been developed with one goal in mind: to help you understand how a living-foods diet can bolster your well-being and longevity—one body system at a time. Each chapter reinforces the concept that healing and vitality emanate from a body that's not only in *balance* but also supported 100 percent by every choice you make.

To help you navigate these concepts, *Healing with Raw Foods* is divided into three Parts that you can tap into no matter where you are on your journey. These sections contain a total of 12 chapters, all designed with specific content to support healing through food.

— Part I, "Getting Started," demonstrates that there are fundamentals to everything in life, including living a high-energy raw-foods lifestyle. Chapter 1, "Mapping a New Way: The 'Why' and 'How' of Eating Raw," explains what you need to know about this lifestyle to be successful. It presents some of the science behind the incredible feeling your body can experience when it's nourished correctly at its core. Chapter 2, "The Living-Foods Kitchen," introduces the foods you'll enjoy in exploring this remarkable lifestyle, with reference to a back-of-the-book Appendix of utensils for making prep in any kitchen a breeze. Chapter 3, "Healing Basics: The Three-Day Jump Start," will help you jump-start your new cuisine with a three-day meal plan. It addresses the one question I get asked the most often: "How do I get started now?"

— Part II, "Healing from Head to Toe," examines specific health systems in your body. Besides exploring how raw foods can positively affect the brain, immune system, heart, musculoskeletal system, and digestive system, these chapters take a look at the impact of this diet approach on diabetes. Each chapter offers recipes I've created to make your healing journey not only effective but also delicious! The choices I've included are designed to stimulate the health of individual systems, while inspiring your best culinary efforts. We've seen tremendous results from these dishes over the past seven years among our 118 Degrees customers. (I look forward to hearing your success story, too!)

— Part III, "Healing the Whole," looks at potential steps for continuing your living-foods journey. Chapter 11, "Healthy Children, Healthy Families," offers food tips and ideas for nurturing growing children. I've tested them in my home kitchen with the other families that I teach, and I can say with confidence that they're "kid approved." Finally, Chapter 12 tackles that most elusive of challenges in "Food for a Healthy Soul."

Recipes and More

Healing with Raw Foods is more than just a collection of recipes, how-to lists, and charts for mastering the basics, even though I've included resources throughout the chapters and in several appendices. It's also a guide to living *holistically*— that is, using food and your meal plan as the starting point for overall health and wellness. By looking at what you eat in the context of your entire well-being rather than isolating your dietary choices, you'll experience positive results for body, mind, *and* spirit.

In short, this is not just another cookbook. It's a wellness manual! As such, I've even included simple affirmations throughout the book to keep you motivated and focused as you transition to your new dietary lifestyle. Just as your body is nourished by high-quality foods, so should your mind be fed by positive, nurturing thoughts that tip the scales in your favor. Affirmations can support you by helping you stay aligned with your highest good, especially if you're tested in your commitment to a new healing path.

I realize that this new eating lifestyle may at first seem strange, confusing, and downright challenging, especially if you're already battling a health issue. You may even question that science supports an enzyme-rich, alkaline raw diet to bolster the human body. But it has been my experience—after 15 years of success with this diet—that when you choose your foundational foods as close to nature as possible, you *will* fortify your body against disease, you *will* strengthen your mind, and you *will* invigorate your spirit. And by generating positive, loving, and supportive thoughts around your choices, you'll enjoy the whole-person benefits of what you eat.

To explain what I mean, I've tapped several medical professionals, doctors noted for their research or work in advanced health and healing principles, to specifically show how changing your relationship with food impacts every aspect of your well-being. They offer some of the growing science behind this miraculous approach to diet and lifestyle. Even though much of the research in this area has focused on overall vegetarian or vegan eating styles, the sum of that work suggests that plant-based foods are emerging as a core target in our understanding of how the body is best supported for optimal health. I've been honored to interview and learn from these forward-thinking individuals. Their eye-opening work has only furthered the truths I have experienced on my own healing path.

Living cuisine, as a whole, actually builds on the path encouraged by many professional organizations and even federal agencies to eat a balanced diet rich in plant-based foods rather than high-fat and processed choices. In its *Dietary Guidelines for Americans 2010*, the USDA's Center for Nutrition Policy and Promotion not only highlights the nutrient benefits of fruits, vegetables, and whole grains but also points to the potential links between eating healthy ingredients and lowering your risk for heart disease and other chronic ailments. Even though the USDA may include other foods and cooking methods in its "balanced" approach, it still acknowledges plant-based ingredients as an important cornerstone of wellness.

My experience has taught me that choosing a living-foods diet strengthens your hand for reaching any number of health goals. It provides the building blocks for great nutrition and cleansing your body. You'll be amazed by how items rich in nutrients and alive in vital energy can make you feel physically *and* mentally restored. I promise! Let the adventure begin . . .

PART ONE

Getting

STARTED

CHAPTER 1

MAPPING A NEW WAY: THE "WHY" AND "HOW" OF EATING RAW

If you could draw a dietary lifestyle map for a healthy future, what would it look like? Would it take you into familiar territory or down previously unexplored paths? Would you meander past old landmarks or point yourself in new directions? Not surprisingly, charting a better course for anything in life, especially your well-being, usually means changing old patterns and mapping new strategies. But when it comes to eating, it's not always easy to steer in a different direction. Just the thought of tossing those comfort foods and other favorites to the wayside can stop you before you take your first step.

But here's something to keep in mind as you go forward: Every bite and morsel you consume has the power to either strengthen and revitalize your body or diminish it. Unfortunately, we don't always think of food in terms of health and healing, even though science consistently points to a link between traditional North American dietary patterns and an epidemic of serious medical issues—heart disease, diabetes, obesity, and even some cancers. Too many of us live casually from meal to meal without considering how our choices impact our bodies. Yet they do! What we eat can be the first line of defense against fatigue, disease, and other stressors that take a toll on our systems over time.

So how can *living cuisine*—foods prepared and eaten as close to their natural state as possible—help you achieve such optimal health and healing? More specifically, why are raw or whole plant-based foods—the heart of this meal plan—the best dietary choice for many humans? I believe by simply re-mapping your choices, you can re-map your life. You can create a new physical experience as it relates to your daily diet. A living-cuisine food plan and lifestyle can be a powerful path to great health because it's based on foods designed by nature as perfect fuels and healing sources. It also focuses on mending mind and spirit as well as body.

The ingredients used throughout this book reconnect us to our food-as-fuel roots. As the first culinary option available to human beings, the raw-food path to healing is as old as life on the planet itself. Ancient texts, such as the Bible, even refer to "releasing energy" by sprouting foods and vegetables, and tinctures made from "herbs of the land." For Hippocrates and other ancient Greek healers, health was a holistic endeavor. Wellness didn't involve treating symptoms; rather, it focused on restoring balance to the body with fresh foods and herbs. Centuries later many people have lost touch with these concepts. We've forgotten the importance of what we eat in promoting good health. Because many of us live in cities, we have little, if any, connection to the raw sources of our food supply. Moreover, we're more likely to concentrate on the social aspects of what we eat rather than its power in fueling our bodies or restoring balance and good health.

Yet raw or plant-based items are full of essential vitamins, minerals, and other nutrients necessary to support your vital organs and systems, as well as repair and reverse, rather than cause, damage to your cells. The trillions of microscopic structures that make up the body—your cells—are constantly at work, replenishing and creating balance so that every organ and system works to your life-affirming benefit.

Whether you want to improve your energy levels or tackle a single health issue, living-foods cuisine can help restore wellness and facilitate healing. By making nutritious choices devoid of the toxins present in other foods, you'll experience tremendous tangible results. The immediate and long-term benefits of awakening your taste buds to exciting new options include weight loss, improved digestion, lowered cholesterol, better blood pressure, increased energy, and enhanced physical endurance. Moreover, you'll find relief from many health conditions, such as ulcers, indigestion, headaches, chronic fatigue, and depression, which are repeatedly linked to poor diets. Some benefits may even help you avert cancer. But you'll also reap rewards in other important, perhaps even unexpected, ways.

A living-foods lifestyle can lead to sharpened mental clarity, balanced emotions, heightened self-awareness, and even a healthy glow.

As amazing as the benefits sound, how does this diet really work? Let's take a closer look.

Science Joins Nature

There are many reasons why living-foods cuisine can help you achieve optimal health and healing. The chemistry and physics behind this dietary plan make it superb for promoting strength and wellness while fighting disease.

Plant-based selections—the foundation of a raw-foods diet—are free of the additives, chemicals, hormones, and other preservatives found in processed and animal-based foods. As such, they don't create the harmful *acidic* environment in which disease thrives. Instead, this eating style encourages a low-toxin, "clean" diet that boosts an *alkaline* or neutral environment in which disease can't thrive. (Chemically speaking, *acidity* and *alkalinity* are measured on a pH or "potential of hydrogen" scale, with 0 to 6 as acidic, 7 as neutral, and 14 as totally alkaline. Nutrient- and enzyme-rich raw or living foods help achieve the neutral to moderately alkaline level your body needs to prevent disease. We'll explore this concept more in Chapter 4.)

Raw foods are full of high-density nutrients, packaged by nature so the body can use them efficiently. By supplying essential vitamins, minerals, proteins, amino acids, and other components, they help maintain vital organs and optimal health. These nutrients have added value in that they also assist in detoxifying or ridding your body of harmful substances. They restore vital balance conducive to good health.

Besides delivering essential nutrients, plant-based foods are also rich in *enzymes*, protein molecules or catalysts necessary for keeping the body running efficiently. The enzymes involved in digestion break down food into nutrients of all sorts so they can be used effectively. Although our bodies produce their own enzymes, it's a finite reserve. You need help from other sources. The abundant supplement offered by plant-based foods helps process nutrients efficiently so the body can go about maintaining vital organs and promoting good health.

Also, unlike traditional high-temperature heating methods, which can break down essential vitamins, minerals, and enzymes as well as create by-products toxic to your health, the raw foods in this diet are never heated above 118°F. That means none of their wholesome nature is removed or "killed" by cooking. Instead, this temperature guarantees the healthiest and biggest nutritional boost possible! I even named my California restaurants 118 Degrees because I believe strongly in preparing our cuisine in such a way that we maintain that same wholesome nature and living energy of every ingredient.

Why Buy Organic?

Although focusing on nature's bounty for nutrients is at the heart of this dietary plan, I encourage you to go one step further and purchase organic when possible. To earn that designation, fruits, vegetables, and other plant-based items are grown, harvested, and processed according to strict USDA guidelines. (Other bodies, such as Oregon Tilth, issue even more closely regulated standards and guidelines for organic products.) That means they're not only raised free of synthetic pesticides, chemical fertilizers, and other toxins but also grown in ways that protect natural resources. By using environmentally friendly methods to manage crops and the land, organic farmers hearken back to traditional farming practices that emphasize and support quality produce grown naturally.

Despite such approaches, few nutrition topics are debated as intensely today as the health benefits of organically grown food. Admittedly, some research disputes the notion that organic ingredients have a nutritional or safety edge over conventionally grown produce. Other studies, however, counter that these fruits and vegetables are nutrient dense because they're generally free of the synthetic pesticides that pose damaging health risks. I believe plant-based foods do benefit from a controlled, pristine growing environment, as well as regulated processing.

To better understand and weigh the merits of organic, however, I recommend visiting the USDA's website, www.usda.gov, as well as the Washington, D.C.–based Environmental Working Group's (EWG) website, www.ewg.org. EWG will help you stay abreast of modern organic agricultural practices and stay alert to foods that are heavily modified. (Organic foods in the U.S. can't be genetically modified, or altered at the gene or DNA level in the laboratory, to produce more desirable traits in a next generation plant. They can be hybridized, however. That is, two purebred varieties of a plant are cross-pollinated or bred to yield an improved variation.) Because organic can be more expensive than traditional produce, a good place to start is by visiting the site's "Clean 15" and "Dirty Dozen" lists to make the best use of your dollar. They're updated yearly as farming methods improve.

Buying organic is not a prerequisite for living-foods cuisine. Yet by being selective in your plant-based choices whenever and wherever possible, you avoid exposing your body to potential toxins. Relying on the healthiest options available will help you harness the best possible result for your overall health. And here's the bonus: Don't worry that raw foods will ever be boring. You'll discover from the recipes in these pages that a living-foods diet takes eating to its delicious, culinary edge.

Alive in Living Energy

For many of us, it's just common sense that a plant-based diet is healthier for your body than a diet of chemically laced or traditionally processed options. But now specialized Kirlian photography, which can actually capture the energy field around an object, gives further credence to the notion that raw foods, particularly those grown organically, produce many life-sustaining benefits because they really are alive and contain their own signature electromagnetic frequencies.

This technique reveals measurable differences in the auras or halos emitted by raw versus cooked or otherwise treated food. The images show that organic selections have an energy flow that is substantially more vibrant and balanced than the uneven and reduced flows produced by traditional foods.

Why is this important? If energy is truly indicative of a food's vitality, then it stands to reason that we'll receive more life-giving sustenance by eating items that emit the highest possible auras. That means ridding our diets of overprocessed and pesticide-ridden foods in favor of organic selections that are "alive" and as close as possible to the way nature intended them. That's reflected in their energy field.

But do raw foods ever lose vitality? The energy flow of living foods lasts for at least six weeks and in many cases longer once they're harvested. As long as you buy, prepare, and eat your choices via the living-foods way, you can enjoy their nutrient benefits for many days.

Plant Strong

Where does a raw diet fit with other plant-based dietary patterns, such as eating vegetarian or vegan? Although these diets are members of the same extended food family—including relatives who don't eat meat, poultry, or seafood—there's considerable variation in what each of these "cousins" deems acceptable. Lacto-ovo-vegetarians, for instance, add eggs and dairy products to their list of grains, vegetables, fruits, legumes, seeds, and nuts. Lacto-vegetarians, on the other hand, appreciate the dairy but not the eggs. As for vegans and raw foodists, even though they're branches of the same vegetarian family, they, too, have their own unique characteristics. Vegan menu choices, for example, can include heavy pastas, processed "fake" meat dishes, soy cheese substitutes, and other similar items.

The important point to remember about how a raw-food eating style differs from other vegetarian versions is that it focuses entirely on nonprocessed foods, free of additives and prepared without standard cooking methods. With raw or living cuisine, each dish consists of fresh, whole plant-based choices that are rich in enzymes and other nutrient values. There's nothing processed or artificial in this diet—or this book. Everything in a raw-foods diet is functional, chosen for its healing properties. No ingredients are added that won't in some way help the body achieve optimal wellness. Even the sea salts you see mentioned in many recipes are a valuable source of trace minerals! Also, I advocate cooking or preparation techniques that bring out the best in a dish without compromising any intrinsic health benefits of the ingredients. Foods are functional building blocks. With every bite, you add something nutritious to your body while satisfying your taste buds.

Choices and Preparation Take Center Stage

By altering your lifestyle to include living foods, you'll be changing your relationship with what you eat. You'll be looking at each item for its health benefits and ability to actually heal your body, rather than because it tastes good. (Not that the selections won't do both!) The key to healing success will be in making food choices based on their nutritional value *and* preparing them in ways that won't harm vital ingredients.

That doesn't mean, however, that exploring can't be fun. In fact, while it will take work to retool your diet, it can also be a culinary adventure into new, vibrant ingredients and recipes. The key to navigating this new path is to focus on what you're adding to your diet and not what you're taking away. This book is chock-full of colorful and nutrient-rich options that incorporate many health-giving ingredients in a single dish. At the same time, they're created to inspire your senses of sight, taste, and even smell. Yes, some of the items may be unfamiliar. In the beginning you may even feel a natural resistance to such finds as sea vegetables and sesame paste (also known as tahini). But you'll likely recognize old standards such as tomatoes, cilantro, and other pantry favorites now packaged in my simple, fun, and functional recipes.

Even though you'll want to select foods as close to their natural state as possible, a raw-foods diet doesn't mean just celery stalks, carrots sticks, or other uncooked fare. In fact, your plan should be a combination of prepared as well as unprepared fruits, vegetables, and other plant-based sources. The mole enchiladas, butternut ravioli, and toffee brownie bites we serve at 118 Degrees, for instance, reflect a gourmet style of preparation that you'll find in the pages of this book. Although you may gravitate to some tastes and textures over others, think of each ingredient, especially those new to your palate, as value-added for your body. I encourage you to start with the flavors you already enjoy and add from there. In time, you'll see how easy it is to create with these new preparation techniques. Much like riding a bike, with just a few tries it will become second nature. You'll be amazed by the goodness of Mother Nature's bounty—and the ease of preparing dishes from it in your own kitchen!

Living Whole

Living cuisine involves living *holistically*—that is, committing to an entire physical, spiritual, and emotional reawakening to support your new diet. *Healing with Raw Foods* isn't just about a new dietary plan that has you eating organic vegetables or drinking green juice every day. Far from it! It's about the interface between your physical health and mental, emotional, and even spiritual well-being. By incorporating strategies that promote the miraculous interconnection between body, mind, and soul, you facilitate healing in the broadest possible way. What might those life-affirming tactics include? A daily "diet" of exercise, affirmations, and other activities—such as yoga, meditation, and journaling—will keep you focused and centered, not to mention invigorated and strong.

As a wife, mother, business owner, and chef, I know how difficult it is to juggle tasks in a busy day, let alone facilitate regular times for personal reflection and connecting with others. It's sometimes a luxury none of us feel we have. But even for the busiest among us, taking a five-minute break here and there to reconnect and get centered is still doable. Although this book doesn't outline instructions for journaling and other meditative tasks, I find them to be natural extensions of the affirmations I do provide.

Once you commit to living whole, you'll find many simple ways to incorporate any of my suggestions or those from other sources. For instance, in addition to starting my morning by reading a few pages of inspirational verse, I build in what I call "gratitude alarms," reminders throughout the day to pause and give thanks. I even program my phone to buzz at 10:04 each morning because it's the time of my birth, a special moment to stop and smell the roses—and to intentionally give thanks for five things I am grateful for in that moment. (What are the significant minutes in the timeline of your life? Set them!) I also step outside frequently just to stretch and breathe fresh air. When I'm waiting for my yoga class to begin, I repeat my favorite affirmations, give thanks for those around me, and pray for wisdom and guidance. It works for other meetings as well! These short segments help me stay balanced.

The point is that you *can* instill the kind of harmony in your life that supports your mental and physical well-being; it really just comes down to how committed you are to making this your new reality. I focus on my spirituality. Perhaps you find peace in your faith, too. I do yoga. Maybe you meditate. I dance in the living room and run barefoot on the lawn. Maybe you walk along the seashore or through the woods. Whatever touchstones make you feel centered, strong, and alive, you need to practice them daily. The important point is to make them part of your day's natural flow, rather than thinking of carving out segments.

If you're taking this journey because of a health crisis, I recommend using the affirmations in this book as a way of gently reminding yourself, particularly in times of stress, of the healing work happening silently inside you. Even though you sometimes can't see or feel the subtle shifts occurring, that doesn't mean that they're not there. Having faith in the miraculous power of your body is an important part of restoring balance and reaching your goals.

Strategies for Big Rewards

I've read that the difference between "interest" and "commitment" is the difference between doing something only when circumstances permit versus doing something when you're determined to see results. No excuses, just action. How true!

But how do you turn the "interest" you may have in living-foods cuisine and a holistic, healthy lifestyle into actual "commitment"? Like me, you probably have many questions as you try to redefine what works for you: *What should I do first in transforming my diet? Where do I shop? How do I know whether a food is really the right food? Will this be a boring diet I can sustain?* There are many tools you can incorporate into your daily life to keep you on the path. In *Healing with Raw Foods* I offer a basic template for launching your new eating style, but keep these quick tips in mind:

— **Be prepared.** If you don't have the necessary ingredients on hand, it will be all too easy to fall back into old patterns and eat whatever is in the house. So make a list and stock your pantry. Do your shopping one day and spend an hour or so preparing your separates the next so you're not stressed when executing your menus. It's easy to become so involved with the details that you forget to enjoy the experience. But remember, *functional* begins with the word *fun*! The process should be a *fun* exploration of new food possibilities. It's not rocket science!

— **Be creative!** The look of food is just as important to your senses as the taste, no matter what you're eating. So make sure the dishes you serve appeal to the eye. Drizzle sauces and add color with parsley sprigs or slices of citrus. Also, achieving optimal digestion with this new diet requires adventure; don't be afraid to explore and make trades as you go along. If you don't like mango, for instance, swap it for a piece of pineapple.

— **Network with others who support you.** A holistic medical provider, for instance, can offer alternative therapies to augment your food and lifestyle choices. He or she will keep you centered as well, especially when life gets in the way. Also, let your friends and family know that you're embarking on a new culinary journey. If you have plans to go out for lunch or dinner, surf the Web for the restaurant's menu so you know what you can eat. Just about any restaurant offers a healthy salad.

— **Be ready for the naysayers.** Not everyone will appreciate your new adventure. Face it . . . the standard American diet (SAD) is the way many people eat and live. But there's an easy way to deal with those who doubt your new choices. When you're questioned, either keep it short with a simple "I'm doing something exciting and new for my continued health" or explode with details as to how this diet has proven right for you. In either case, to be forewarned is to be forearmed, even if it's regarding food. You won't win over everyone, but maybe you'll plant a living-cuisine seed!

— **Keep a journal.** Writing down how you feel at a particular moment or on a certain day allows you to connect your living-foods lifestyle with your body's response while evaluating your progress. A good place to begin is by listing your personal expectations, successes, and failures as you move through what I call the Three-Day Jump Start into your daily dietary plan. Which foods were easy to prepare or satisfying to your palate? Which would you avoid at all costs? How did you feel emotionally and physically when you began this journey? Perhaps sluggish and unhappy? How are you doing now? Hopefully, energized and restored. As you transition your diet, you may have doubts. That's okay; it's common when your energy drops or you're working through detoxification. But that's when you need journaling the most. Use it to uncover the truths that mirror and reinforce the real you!

— **Reflect. Reflect. Reflect.** Sometimes it's hard to see your progress amid the chaos of life or the negativity of others who don't understand your path or have a different framework for your choices. But an important part of a living-foods cuisine and a holistic lifestyle is to reflect routinely on your growth as you focus on the healing task at hand. Life is never perfect, but there's beauty in the smallest steps, especially the ones that move you forward toward your dietary and wellness goals. Enjoy them!

Focus on Adding

Use these strategies to focus on adding more of these healing foods into your diet and lifestyle. After enjoying a diet comprising at least 50 percent living foods, you will begin to notice a marked improvement in your health. Many people report simple things like increased clarity; others report reversing health conditions completely. The more you add, the better you will feel. If you are in a healing crisis, consider making your diet at least 80 percent living foods so that you can effectively stimulate the body to heal quickly, restoring health. As a rule of thumb for an ongoing vibrant lifestyle, remember to keep the balance. The upcoming chapters contain tools to guide you on where to start, so that the science behind the healing power of these foods can go to work for you right away.

A Final Note

Now that you've read how living cuisine can change your life in positive ways, it's time to get down to basics. Every journey, especially one toward improved health and wellness, involves strategies and preparation to map an effective course. The best first steps are to familiarize yourself with a few fundamentals that will make your trip easier and more productive. With this eating approach, shopping and prepping are everything. The more you plan and execute in advance, the more efficient and jazzed you'll be with your new eating style. In Chapter 2, "The Living-Foods Kitchen," we look at the foods and ingredients you'll need to be successful.

THE LIVING-FOODS KITCHEN

Unless you're already familiar with living cuisine, you may be new to many of the ingredients that make up this lifestyle. A raw-foods diet is unique among others in that it goes beyond traditional fruits, vegetables, and other plant-based ingredients to highlight nutritional sources likely new to your palate. The value-added beauty is that you can eat a lot of food—in fact, the more the better—to get those nutritious benefits! Living-cuisine items are generally low in calories, yet packed with nutritional value.

The secret to success, however, is to keep plenty of choices on hand. Whether you forge ahead aggressively or go slowly, the more nutrient-rich raw items you have in your pantry, the easier it will be to transition to an eating style I believe is both fun and functional. (You may even want to stock your refrigerator and cupboards with doubles and triples of items that have a longer shelf life.) Here's further encouraging news: As your dedication to the diet increases, you'll discover more products to fill the shelves!

Do you need to revamp your entire pantry to jump-start your diet? No, but it's a good idea to begin removing processed and other items that run counter to your new meal plan. All the recipes in this book are free of gluten, wheat, dairy, and, with the exception of unpasteurized miso, soy. What makes these common allergens, likely components in many of the foods you have in your kitchen, bad for you? They're often genetically modified, meaning they've been altered at the plant's cellular level to grow a more resilient crop. Those that aren't modified have been hybridized, or mixed with other plants, in an effort to provide greater crop yields and higher profits.

In either case, manipulating a plant's genetic code changes or mutates its basic structure, which can cause harmful side effects to the body. By focusing on living foods, you take a big step in eliminating those risks. Although *Healing with Raw Foods* contains many different ingredients, I've profiled a few raw foodie staples below. You'll see them frequently and use them repeatedly. Consider them the first means in healing your body.

Building a Healing Pantry

Stocking your pantry with a few living-food basics will provide a great foundation for easy preparation throughout your week. As you scan this cookbook, start with the ingredients and recipes that are most appealing to you. (There's never a good reason to eat foods you don't like!) If you're still uncertain as to a good jumping-off point, keep it simple with one protein-based powder, one raw oil, one nut butter, two to four spice blends, and some nori sheets. They can be combined easily with fresh produce to create a quick raw meal or snack.

If you want a few more ingredients for those first smoothies, sauces, and wraps, I suggest adding several types of nuts and seeds, fresh coconut or coconut oil/butter, cold-pressed extra-virgin olive oil, sea salt, and a healthy sweetener. They're part of the bigger ingredient families you'll eventually work into your diet. They may not be too familiar right now, but read further for a quick look at the possibilities.

— **Coconut and nut butters.** A densely nutritious spread used in creamy sauces, breakfast items, and desserts, coconut butter is pureed from unadulterated whole coconut flesh with no additives. It's a slightly sweet source of healthy fats, dietary fiber, protein, vitamins, and minerals. Although coconut is technically a seed, it's part of a whole category of nut butters, which also include organic almonds, cashews, pecans, macadamias, walnuts, and other nuts. In addition to being used for shortcut milks and nut butters, coconut butter can turn any smoothie into a meal by providing an extra source of protein, along with essential vitamins and minerals.

Source: The nut butter and oil section of any health food store. My favorite products carry the label Artisana.

Storage: Once opened, refrigerate.

— **Coconut flesh.** The inside fruit portion of a popular tropical fruit, coconut flesh is a great multipurpose ingredient. My recipes usually call for young Thai coconut, fruit that's indigenous to both Thailand and its cuisine. "Young" simply indicates that the coconut has been harvested before it's fully mature, making the mottled green-brown husks tender and easy to crack. The coconut shreds and milk, however, aren't lacking in flavor. They offer a delightful taste for any number of dishes. To achieve a creamy butter-like texture for yogurts, frostings, and other crèmes, blend the contents. To use as a meat substitute in tacos, wraps, and seafood ceviches or appetizers, strip and clean the fruit under warm running water to remove any husk chards, and then slice or dice.

Source: Asian markets and health food stores.

Storage: Up to two weeks in the refrigerator if fresh at the time of purchase. (To ensure freshness, avoid black, purple, or brown dried, discolored husks.) The flesh can be refrigerated for up to three days after being removed from the husk.

— **Coconut flour.** The dried and ground meat of a coconut, coconut flour provides the basis for many living-cuisine desserts.

Source: Readily available at health food stores. Look for "raw" variety.

Storage: In an airtight container in the pantry indefinitely.

— **Coconut water.** Tapped from a young Thai coconut, coconut water is a perfect liquid for smoothies and other recipes requiring aroma and sweetness. Each coconut yields from 8 to 16 ounces that can be enjoyed as a refreshing chilled drink or blended into various recipes.

Source: Asian or health food stores. (Buy fresh because boxed or other packaged coconut water is pasteurized at high heat, which results in higher sugar content. It's therefore not considered "raw.")

Storage: Refrigerate liquid for up to three days.

— **Fresh milks (almond or seed).** Created by blending almonds with water, raw almond milk is a satisfying substitute for cow's milk. Its health benefits stem from a high protein content, without the saturated fat or lactose of dairy milk. Because almond milk is made from nuts, it's obviously not acceptable for people with nut allergies. (Substitute hemp, sesame, pumpkin, sunflower, or other seed milks.) But for anyone else, it can be used in recipes, on cereal, or as the base of a smoothie. With a flavor often preferable to soy or rice milk, raw almond milk is also tasty straight from the glass.

Source: Health food stores. Can be made at home by soaking almonds overnight and then straining them and pureeing them with water in a blender. For a quick milk version, combine water with nut butters and simply blend. (See recipe on page 42.)

Storage: In the refrigerator for up to five days.

— **Gluten-free grains.** In a raw-foods diet, you'll want to use grains sparingly, balancing them with fresh produce to create a diet that's alkaline and anti-inflammatory, particularly in terms of the digestive tract. Buckwheat and quinoa (pronounced *keen-wah*) fit the bill, in large part because they lack gluten, the protein-based substance linked to other grains such as rye, barley, and especially wheat. Both are technically seeds and not grains, which is good news for the body in terms of its ability to metabolize them. Used liberally in processed baked goods and other foods to add texture and flavor, gluten can result in a common allergic reaction called gluten intolerance. Sprouted buckwheat and quinoa, on the other hand, are excellent ingredients for dehydrated breads, crackers, and toppings. Besides being a source of protein and complex carbohydrates for energy, these grains don't create undue stress on the digestive tract. Instead, their nutrient value is easily absorbed.

Varieties: Even though they're technically seeds, buckwheat and quinoa are the easiest gluten-free grains to use and digest.

Source: Health food stores (for bulk purchases) as well as grocery stores.

Storage: Refrigerate and use within three days after sprouting.

— **Miso (unpasteurized).** A part of Japanese cuisine for centuries, miso is a fermented paste made from unpasteurized soybeans, cultured grains, and sea salt. It contains a natural digestive enzyme called *lactobacillus* and other helpful microorganisms that aid in healthy digestion by destroying harmful bacteria. It also contains carbohydrates, protein, essential oils, minerals, vitamins, and amino acids.

Although miso comes in various colors, based on the final ingredient content during fermentation, I recommend two versions: White miso is made from soybeans fermented with rice, resulting in a sweet taste that's wonderful for condiments, dressings, or light sauces. Red miso is typically fermented from soybeans, barley, or other grains. Because the flavor can be intense, it's perfect for hearty soups and sauces. With its living microorganisms, unpasteurized miso should be used sparingly. However, this form of soy is considered a generally acceptable, delicious, all-purpose, high-protein food.

Source: Health food stores' refrigerated sections. Look for options labeled "non-GMO," indicating that it's from a non–genetically modified organism.

Storage: In the refrigerator according to package directions.

— **Nuts and seeds.** Basic ingredients in many of the sauces featured in *Healing with Raw Foods*, nuts and seeds are a healthy source of protein for energy and essential fatty acids (EFAs), fats that the body needs but can't produce on its own. (You're likely familiar with omega-3, but perhaps less familiar with omega-6 or omega-9 fatty acids, which are also necessary.) I recommend pumpkin seeds for adrenal gland support, walnuts for the brain, almonds for healthy digestion, and hemp seeds for an easy way to boost the protein of any meal (14 grams in just 2 tablespoons!). Flaxseeds aid in elimination and brain development.

Varieties: Besides the options above, pecans, pistachios, and macadamia nuts as well as sesame, sunflower, and chia seeds make for crunchy, nutritious alternatives.

Source: Health food stores.

Storage: In airtight containers in the pantry, out of direct light, or in the freezer. Storage time depends on freshness when purchased. In general, I recommend buying nuts monthly and using them immediately. If you have leftovers after 30 days, make sure you use them within the next two weeks or discard.

— **Oils.** Although oils are a necessary component of a living-cuisine diet for their essential fatty acids, you must be selective. Raw oils typically haven't been heated at high temperatures during the extraction process, so they maintain their nutritional value. Higher-quality raw oils are labeled "extra-virgin, cold-pressed," "first cold extracted," or "raw." Raw oils provide an excellent base for dressings and marinades. But FYI: Make sure you enjoy the flavor of the oil you select. Because you won't be sautéing with it, the taste will translate into your final dish.

Varieties: Typical examples include olive oil, hemp oil, flax oil, coconut oil, and avocado oil.

Source: Health food stores for the best selection.

Storage: Because light and air are oil's enemies, store selections in an airtight container with a tight-fitting lid in a dark cupboard. Although most oils can be kept in the pantry, flaxseed oil should be refrigerated. Raw oils should be used within a month of opening the container.

— **Olives.** As a source of vitamin E, olives are a welcome addition to a raw-foods diet. They can be used in many different ways: as a snack and garnish as well as an essential oil in a salad, sauce, or entrée. Olives are the delicious stand-out ingredient in the Live Chopped Veggie Salad (page 236).

Varieties: Olives come in many varieties, from black to green, whole to pitted, and Sicilian to kalamata or Greek. For greatest benefits, look for "raw," or "low temperature," meaning they're cured, brined, or treated and packed in olive oil or sea salt and water. Avoid olives brined in distilled vinegar because the solution is somewhat acidic, which counters the health benefits of the olives.

Source: Raw online food suppliers and local health food stores. Also shop your local farmers' markets for regional organic brands. Adams' Olive Ranch is my California go-to source, but there are likely options in your area of the world.

Storage: Refrigerate after opening and use within three to four months.

— **Sea vegetables.** If you think vegetables grow only in soil, consider this delicious and nutritious option. Sea vegetables are algae- or seaweed-based staples that have been a part of Asian and other cuisines for centuries. Because they're grown in the nurturing saline environment of the ocean, at various coastal locations around the world, they provide an excellent source of nutrients, including B vitamins, iron, and many trace minerals found in the sea. More important, because the bloodstream easily absorbs the minerals contained in sea vegetables, these foods can be considered a daily mineral source or supplement in a living-foods diet. Just as there are varied uses for land vegetables, there are varied uses for sea vegetables, from soups and salads to snacks and sandwich wraps.

Varieties: Often referred to generically as seaweed, the sea vegetables dulse, sea lettuce, kelp, laver, and nori are nutrient- and flavor-filled delights that add variety and depth to a raw-foods repertoire:

- *Dulse* or *sea lettuce.* As with other sea vegetables, the fronts or stringy leaves of dulse aren't green. As part of the red marine algae family, they vary from rose to reddish brown to purplish red in their natural state. Look for the purplish hue, however, because it usually denotes that the lettuce hasn't been heat-treated. The best sources of North American dulse and sea lettuce come from the Maine coast. Because dulse has a salty taste, it can stand alone as a snack or be chopped or torn for soups and salads. And because it's available in a shaker, dulse can be easily integrated into any dish. Just sprinkle the flakes for a quick dose of minerals. Sea lettuce has a bit more body and is great added to soups and salads.

- *Kelp.* Harvested from cool coastal underwater forests, kelp is a brownish marine plant available in raw pasta-like noodles or large dried sheets. Kelp's natural salty taste makes it a popular living-cuisine staple. To reconstitute, the sheets are usually cut into bite-size pieces or strips and submerged for ten minutes in lukewarm water before being incorporated into soups and salads.

- *Laver.* Also known as wild Atlantic nori, laver is a North Atlantic cousin to the nori sheets traditionally used in sushi. In its unprocessed form, it can add a variety of flavors—from subtle salty sea taste to slightly sweet or nutty—to soups, salads, and other dishes. Unlike nori sheets, laver must be soaked in lukewarm water before use.

- *Nori sheets.* Nori, the paper-thin wrapping that binds Japan's famous delicacy, is grown in nets so it can be easily harvested before it is processed. Although the sheets come in varied colors and flavors, depending on the type of seaweed used and how it was treated, look for purple, black, and unroasted options. Because of its salty flavor, nori is ideal for rolling up vegetable-, sprout-, and grain-based entrées.

Sources: Asian and health food stores for all sea vegetables.

Storage: In an airtight container in the pantry for dried versions. Refrigerate when cooked.

— **Spices/salts.** Because there are very few raw spices on the market, it's generally acceptable to use conventional dried seasonings. The school of thought is that they don't lose their nutritional benefits even when heated above 118°F. The important point is to buy the freshest products available. Because turmeric is great for memory and cinnamon is a powerful antioxidant, I keep quality sources of both handy. I stock sea and Himalayan pink crystal salts for additional seasoning. Both are acceptable raw foods because they're naturally dried rather than mined, heated, bleached, or otherwise treated as is common table salt. As such, they contain a full spectrum of essential minerals and trace elements necessary for your health. Just make sure any herbs you buy are non-irradiated and organic when possible.

Source: Health food stores or online at Mountain Rose Herb Company (www.mountainroseherbs.com) or www.118degrees.com.

Storage: In an airtight container in the pantry.

BBQ BLEND
(Makes 1 cup)

½ cup dark chili powder

2 tablespoons paprika

2 tablespoons dried onion

2 tablespoons dried garlic

2 tablespoons rosemary

2 tablespoons dried coconut sugar or 1 teaspoon stevia

1 tablespoon salt

Mixing It Up

Variety is the spice of life, even with a raw diet. A curry blend one day and an Italian mix the next not only adds creativity to cooking but also satisfies your palate in different ways. Because cooking is an art, I recommend seasoning to taste with the mixes below.

ITALIAN BLEND
(Makes ¾ cup)

¼ cup dried basil

2 tablespoons dried garlic

2 tablespoons dried onion

2 tablespoons dried rosemary

2 tablespoons dried parsley

SPANISH BLEND
(Makes ¾ cup)

¼ cup dark chili powder

2 tablespoons dried onion

2 tablespoons paprika

2 tablespoons ground chipotle

2 tablespoons oregano

2 tablespoons cayenne pepper

1 tablespoon sea salt

CURRY BLEND
(Makes ½ cup)

¼ cup turmeric

2 tablespoons cumin

2 tablespoons ground yellow mustard seed

1 tablespoon coriander

1 tablespoon dried bay leaf

JENNY'S DESSERT BLEND
(Makes ⅔ cup)

¼ cup cinnamon

2 tablespoons nutmeg

2 tablespoons maca root

2 tablespoons dried ginger

1 tablespoon ground clove

Superfoods and Superstars

Superfoods are a key ingredient for staying healthy and healing holistically. The term describes plant-based items that offer a high phytochemical and antioxidant content in a very compact package. Foods such as broccoli, nuts, and blueberries, common in a traditional diet, are rich in vitamin C, minerals, proteins, and other nutrients. You can achieve great health benefits by eating small amounts of these foods.

In the raw-foods lifestyle, we celebrate those same "super" fruits and vegetables, even though I like to refer to them as "daily essentials" because they should be regular items in any healthy diet. I reserve the term *superfoods* (or even *nutrient superstars*) for a bevy of other whole food–derived supplements that are even more intense in their nutritional payload than many traditional plant-based items.

Here is my golden rule for how to use these nutrient-dense foods for best results in your diet: *the 80/20 rule.*

> Enjoy 80 percent fresh fruits and vegetables in
> every plate or dish, and balance those with 20 percent
> nutrient-dense superfoods and superstars.

You need add only a teaspoon here or a tablespoon there of these green powders, berries, seeds, and other sources to pack the same powerful punch as multiple veggie servings. A teaspoon of spirulina or goji berries, for instance, can be more efficient in reaching your daily intake needs than several servings of broccoli, despite its high vitamin content. Similarly, 2 tablespoons of hemp seeds provide the same complete protein as an 8-ounce piece of chicken. So which living-food supplements can deliver huge rewards in small nutrient packages? Check out the nutrient superstars below.

— **Cacao nibs.** Also known as raw chocolate, these living-food superfoods are bits of cocoa beans harvested from the evergreen *Theobroma cacao* tree. Cultivated in Mexico and South America centuries before its fruit became known to Europe and North America, the cacao tree yields seeds from leathery pods that eventually grow into beans. They're harvested, fermented, dried, and then broken into sweet raw "nibs" prior to roasting.

Although raw chocolate was treasured by ancient civilizations for its medicinal attributes, its full health benefits today are still under investigation. It's known, however, to be very high in certain antioxidants, minerals, and essential fatty acids. Besides possibly raising good cholesterol and lowering bad choles-terol, raw cacao is a natural stimulant linked to enhanced moods. Crunchy and flavorful, nibs are similar to unsweetened baker's chocolate, yet richer in taste. They can be used in any raw-food dessert, smoothie, or other recipe. I also eat them by the handful, often for breakfast.

Source: Health food stores and online.

Storage: In an airtight container in the pantry.

— **Carob.** With its unique, sweet flavor, carob is a delicious living-foods substitute for cocoa. Carob originates as a seed or legume of a centuries-old evergreen shrub, native to the Mediterranean and now growing in warm U.S. climates. The seeds form in bean-like pods, which are dried, roasted, and ground into a cocoa-like powder and further formulated into chips. Unlike chocolate, carob boasts a host of nutrients: protein; vitamins A, B_1, B_2, B_3, and D; and cal-cium, along with other minerals. Although carob's taste is often compared to chocolate, it actually has an earthy, caramel or coffee-like flavor (much like the Tootsie Rolls from my own childhood!). It's great in smoothies, desserts, and other dishes. Because carob is naturally sweet, a little goes a long way.

Source: Health food stores and online.

Storage: In an airtight container in the pantry.

— **Goji berries.** Known to be extremely rich in vitamin C and other antiox-idants, goji berries are also sources of nutrients: vitamins E, B_1, B_2, and B_6; cal-cium; magnesium; 18 amino acids; and protein. The fruit of evergreen bushes, these small dried berries have been a Chinese and Tibetan herbalist mainstay for centuries, even though their modern-day health benefits are still being in-vestigated. They add a tart, raisin-like flavor to salads, trail mixes, crusts, and desserts. They also can be soaked for tea.

Source: Online or through health food stores. Check the bulk section for best pricing.

Storage: In an airtight container in the pantry.

— **Hemp.** Rich in omega-3, omega-6, and omega-9 fatty acids as well as other nutrients, hemp protein powder is considered a complete protein in that it supplies the essential protein-triggering amino acids the body needs but can't produce on its own. Hemp is an easily digested and effective substitute for animal-based protein in a living-foods diet. Two tablespoons of the powder pro-vide 14 grams of protein to smoothies, sauces, soups, or other dishes. Because of its nutrients, hemp is linked to multiple health benefits, from building muscle to fighting degenerative free radicals in the cells.

I recommend protein-complex powder blends as a balanced alternative to hemp powder alone because they combine multiple plant sources. Healthforce Nutritionals' Warrior Food protein, for instance, is formulated from a base of hemp and pea protein and balanced with a probiotic blend and nopal cactus, aka prickly pear cactus, for, respectively, greater assimilation and metabolic and blood sugar support. Hemp seeds and hemp butter are also significant protein sources.

Source: Health food stores or online.

Storage: In an airtight container in the pantry.

— **Maca root powder.** Similar to a turnip, the maca plant is native to the Peruvian Andes. Sun dried and pounded into a powder, the root contains more than 55 phytochemicals as well as B vitamins and amino acids known to boost energy and endurance. (*Phyto-* means "plant based.") With its nutrient concentration, maca root is reputed to stimulate hormone production and help regulate the adrenal glands, thereby enhancing natural energy. Maca root powder adds a slightly caramel flavor to smoothies and desserts.

Source: Health food stores or through my website, 118degrees.com. (I offer a special wild-crafted organic variety imported from Peru.)

Storage: In an airtight container in the pantry.

— **Seeds.** It's not hard to see why chia and flaxseeds have been identified as superfoods; they're rich in multiple nutrients. Chia seeds (yes, the same ones that grow "fur" on the Chia Pet!) are high not only in fiber but also in calcium, omega-3 fatty acids, and amino acids. Flaxseeds, which are similarly nutrient endowed, perform many health functions, particularly in protecting the heart. Whether you're drawn to nutty-flavored flaxseeds or neutral-flavored chia seeds, you'll find many uses for these "super" options. Sprinkle them on salads, blend them into smoothies, or mix them into soup.

Source: Health food stores or online.

Storage: In an airtight container in the pantry.

— **Supergreen powders.** Supergreen powders are a nutrient must-have in your pantry because they contain a concentration of vital vitamins and minerals. They're derived from dark leafy greens harvested from select land or water sources and processed with state-of-the-art methods into powders or other forms.

What makes these supplements especially potent is the presence of chlorophyll, the green pigment that gives plants color. In the human body, chlorophyll has been shown to aid in stimulating new cell growth while also repairing damaged cells. Along with its other disease-fighting properties, chlorophyll neutralizes toxins, which explains green powder juice's successful role in detoxification and delivering nutrients directly into the bloodstream.

Even though there are many concentrated green products on the market, each formulation is unique in its nutrient content and targets. As you become more comfortable eating the living-foods way, you'll likely become more familiar with each selection. Whatever you choose, it's good to incorporate one green complex into your daily diet for its wholesome, nutritional benefits. For starters, I suggest:

- *Spirulina*. Offering the nutrient punch of concentrated greens, this powder supplement is a product of blue-green algae grown in a controlled saline or ocean-water environment. It contains 60 percent protein plus B_{12}, iron, beta-carotene, chlorophyll, and GLA, an essential fatty acid. Spirulina can be added to smoothies as a nutritional booster or integrated into sauces and desserts, such as the Spirulina Shake on page 74.

    Source: Local health food stores and online.
    Storage: In an airtight container in the pantry.

- *E3Live*. The basis for this dietary supplement is wild *Aphanizomenon flos-aquae* (AFA) blue-green algae. Harvested from Oregon's Upper Klamath Lake, one of the richest freshwater nutrient sources in the world, the algae used in E3Live is rich in chlorophyll, vitamin B_{12}, omega-3 fatty acids, and 22 amino acids. I recommend E3Live frozen liquid to ensure potency. Once thawed, mix into a fruit smoothie or dilute in water or green juice.

    Source: Health food stores or online at www.E3Live.com.
    Storage: Freeze.

- *Dr. Schulze's SuperFood Plus*. Superfood complexes provide intense phytonutrient content in a simple-to-use powder formulation. The most effective of these complexes contain absorbable nutrients from land and sea. Thus, I recommend SuperFood Plus because it offers the best of both worlds—a complete vitamin and mineral profile from aquatic *and* land grasses. As a whole-foods concentrate, SuperFood Plus boosts your energy while strengthening various systems. It contains your daily dose of water-soluble vitamins, which eliminates the need for an additional daily multivitamin.

Source: Health food stores and online at www.herbdoc.com.
Storage: In an airtight container in the pantry.

Sweeteners

Just because you're eating healthfully with living-food cuisine doesn't mean you still can't satisfy your sweet tooth. A raw-foods diet features many substitutes—raw honey, dates, nectars, and other options—for the traditional sweeteners of the standard American diet.

The difference, however, is that these natural ingredients are free of the onerous features linked to refined or processed sugar, such as "empty" or non-nutrient calories and artificially spiked insulin levels. Such sugars also can be addictive and acidic to the body and produce other deleterious health effects.

Conversely, natural sweeteners are low glycemic, meaning they don't cause small, fleeting rises in your blood sugar but rather sustained energy. Some also may yield essential vitamins and minerals as well as enzymes for better metabolism. Whichever raw sweetener you use from the list that follows, it's important to understand that your body isn't designed to take in a concentrated amount. So for optimal health, use sparingly.

— **Dates.** As ancient as civilization itself, dates are one of the world's oldest cultivated and nutritious fruits. They're a sweet product of the date palm, a tree first indigenous to the desert oases of Africa, southwest Asia, and the Middle East, and now growing in arid areas of the U.S. Known for being antioxidant rich and iron dense, dates are also great sources of dietary fiber and a balanced spectrum of other minerals. As such, they help protect your heart, lower your blood pressure, and even destroy disease-causing free radicals.

From Deglet Noor to Medjool, dates vary based on size, color, texture, and flavor. The caramel-like flavor is perfect in smoothies and cereals; dates can also be pureed in a blender with nuts and other dried fruit for a snack.

Source: Health food stores and online for both fresh and dried.
Storage: In an airtight container in the pantry or refrigerator.

— **Indigenous sweeteners.** Yacon syrup and stevia are regular low-glycemic sugar substitutes in many other cultures, as well as in a living-cuisine diet.

- *Yacon syrup* originates with the succulent leaves of the yacon plant, vegetation indigenous to South America. A sweeter version of molasses, caramel, or honey, yacon syrup needs to be used sparingly and substituted carefully because of its intensity. Although low in calories, it isn't known for its nutrients. Like other natural sweeteners, however, yacon syrup doesn't increase blood sugar levels dramatically.

- *Stevia* is a sweet leaf derived from a shrubby perennial plant native to Paraguay but cultivated in many other parts of the world. Although used as a sugar substitute in Japan and China for decades, it's a relatively recent arrival to North America. Its full health benefits remain unclear. Stevia produces a unique licorice-like flavor with sweetness that can linger much longer than sugar. (In high concentrations, it leaves a bitter aftertaste.) It is available in both powder and liquid drop form. A little stevia goes a long way in smoothies and desserts, and because it's an herb that does not affect insulin, it's the best sweetener for people with sugar sensitivities.

Source: Health food stores and online. I recommend stevia in liquid form for most culinary applications.
Storage: In an airtight container in the pantry.

— **Nectars.** The sweet sap of flowering plants offers another delicious, natural, low-glycemic alternative to refined sugar. Organic nectars are effective recipe substitutes for traditional brown sugar, maple syrup, and even honey in desserts, sauces, and tea. They produce different sweetened flavors based on their source.

- *Sunchoke nectar,* for instance, is made from Jerusalem artichokes, a gnarly tubular plant resembling gingerroot that is native to eastern North America. It yields a rich molasses-like flavor.

- *Coconut nectar,* the dehydrated fragrant sap of coconut palm flowers—the tiny buds that grow into full-fledged coconuts—offers a hint of floral. Unlike refined sugar, this nectar also delivers a spate of vitamins, minerals, and amino acids.

- *Raw agave nectar,* extracted from the hearts of blue agave plants indigenous to the Mexican desert, produces a honey-like flavor, which makes it significantly sweeter than sugar. Like the other nectars, agave is low glycemic but should be used sparingly. I recommend raw dark organic agave because the lighter varieties are processed in such a way that the sugar or fructose content rises.

Source: Health food stores and online.
Storage: In an airtight container in the pantry.

— **Raw local honey.** Although both standard and raw honey share the same beginnings—bees harvest nectar from flowering plants to create it—the two products part ways after the hive. Unlike standard honey, which undergoes a heating and filtering process that destroys much of its nutritional value and subtle flavoring, the locally sourced raw honey in living cuisine remains unadulterated.

Honey that's purchased as close to nature as possible is honey at its flavorful best. It also contains simple carbohydrates and an assortment (albeit in small doses) of vitamins, minerals, and amino acids. Although higher in calories than refined sugar, raw honey is easily converted into glucose, the body's universal energy. A simple sweetener for sauces, smoothies, and desserts, it's also used for aiding digestive challenges.

Source: Local farmers' markets as well as health food stores and online.
Storage: In an airtight container in the pantry.

— **Vanilla bean paste.** A thick, viscous spread created from ground vanilla beans, vanilla bean paste is a popular living-foods alternative to vanilla extract for cooking and baking. Although commercially sold pastes are available, you can make your own by pulverizing vanilla beans into a powder with your spice grinder and then mixing it with raw honey or water until you achieve the desired consistency. (If you start with vanilla pods, you'll need to extract the beans and dry them first. If you want to shortcut the entire process, you can purchase vanilla powder and mix it with the binder.) In either case, the finished product is a suitable sweetener in any dessert, sauce, smoothie, or other recipe that calls for the unique sweet taste of vanilla.

Source: Online or in health food stores.

Storage: Refrigerate vanilla bean paste once opened. Because the paste has about a one-week shelf life, turn vanilla bean powder into small quantities of paste as needed.

Buying Basics and the Power of Four!

Even with the items listed in this chapter, you'll still be making many choices on your own. Once you're comfortable implementing the steps and changes in this book, assessing which products or ingredients are right for your diet will become second nature. You'll know instinctively, for instance, why an organic avocado is naturally better for you than white bread.

Readers familiar with my previous cookbooks know that I refer liberally to the "good stuff" when talking about items that promote healthy well-being. I'm generally referring to ingredients high in live enzymes, healthy fats, fiber, and nutrients of all sorts. But deciding which are "good" nutrient choices can be daunting, especially with so much to learn initially. So if you're in doubt about the "why" behind any given item, ask these four simple questions in making the call. Scoring well in three areas is good, but success in all four wins the day.

1. **What is this food?** If label ingredients—gluten, food coloring, hydrogenated or partially hydrogenated oils, or synthetic nutrients and other additives—suggest a processed item, leave it on the shelf. Conversely, if it's fresh, it's likely full of nutrients—vitamins, minerals, essential fatty acids, and dietary fiber—that will support your daily needs. Put it in your basket.

2. **Did it grow in the ground, on a tree, or in the sea?** Because a raw diet emphasizes foods in a state as close as possible to that which nature intended, you'll want to focus on plant-based items grown organically or in a controlled environment free of pesticides and other toxins. That includes fruits and vegetables along with nuts, seeds, grains, herbs, spices, sea vegetables, and minimally processed products. The simple rule of thumb in making good, nourishing choices is to buy *whole* foods—items that are fresh, organic, and nutrient rich. You want items that come *from* a plant—not produced *in* a plant!

3. **What are the health benefits?** Processed foods are often devoid of necessary nutrients while full of empty calories and additives. They can spike your blood sugar levels, creating an unnatural insulin reaction that leaves you lethargic rather than energized. Whether it's white bread or another high-fat or processed selection, take a pass if the label suggests such negative consequences. Foods that give you energy, keep your weight in healthy check, satisfy your daily nutrient requirements, and/or provide overall nourishment should always garner your attention. Like that avocado, such foods likely contain a plethora of nutrients that feed your body and stimulate your brain.

4. **How was it prepared?** "Raw" in a raw diet generally denotes foods in their natural *uncooked* state, even though you'll likely want to include lightly prepared ones, too. The items that you'll do best to avoid have lost their nutritional value through heavy processing, frying, or other degrading cooking methods. The ones you want to include are fruits, vegetables, and other living-cuisine options served either raw or cooked below 118°F to maintain their nutrient and enzyme strength.

By keeping these four questions in mind when you make your selections, you'll become a savvy raw-food pro!

Quick Prep Techniques and Tips

Many of the recipes in *Healing with Raw Foods* require that you do a quick prep of some ingredients before you start mixing. You'll see repeated references, for instance, to sprouting grains, reconstituting dried fruit, and de-stemming greens. These are actually very simple tasks that, unless otherwise noted, are performed as indicated by the directions below. Also, unless a recipe suggests something different, always pit fresh dates and avocados and remove the leafy stem at the top of strawberries.

— **Sprouting grains.** To optimize the benefits of raw grains, seeds, and nuts, sprout them before use. By releasing surface enzyme inhibitors or shields protecting each morsel as it grows, this simple process significantly boosts protein and vitamin content. More important, it helps with optimal digestion. Although nuts and seeds are rich in nutrients and can be eaten without soaking or sprouting, grains such as buckwheat and quinoa are a different story. These grains sprout quickly, but you'll need to employ some basic techniques to ready them for use. Simply submerge the grains in a container of water for about 12 hours. Then rinse and drain. You'll see a small sprout emerging from the tip of each soft seed. Once they've sprouted, store for up to 3 days in the refrigerator, rinsing and draining once a day. Nuts and seeds can be processed in a similar fashion by soaking them for 1 to 3 days (depending on the nut) or 6 hours to 2 days (depending on the seed). For more detailed information on the art of sprouting grains, nuts, and seeds, see www.sproutpeople.org.

— **Reconstituting dried fruits.** Many of the recipes in this cookbook call for reconstituting dehydrated items. This is an easy process accomplished by first placing items such as sun-dried tomatoes, dates, or figs in a bowl and covering with lukewarm (80° to 100°F) water. After 30 minutes, check the texture of each piece. It should feel soft. Depending on the size, reconstituting may take up to several hours. When pliable, drain and use. Some recipes also call for reconstituted kelp, which can be accomplished by first cutting the kelp into strips and then submerging them in warm water. Check after 10 minutes and thereafter until pliable. Rinse, drain, and use.

— **De-stemming greens.** You'll see references to de-stemming greens throughout this book. Whether you're working with lettuce, chard, spinach, kale, mustard greens, or collard greens, removing the stem can be done efficiently with any of three methods:

1. Lay the leaf stem-side up on a flat surface. Separate the green portion by cutting along each side of the stem in a V.

2. Fold the leaf in half along the stem and lay on a flat surface. Run the knife blade alongside the vein to separate it.

3. Grasp the stem by one hand and pull the leafy portion away with the other hand.

A final FYI on leafy green stems: If they're flexible, they indicate a tender young plant that's good for salads and raw use.

— **De-stemming mushrooms.** Separating the stem of a mushroom from the cap is another simple technique, accomplished with a few easy maneuvers of the hand. Just grasp the stem with your thumb, forefinger, and middle finger. Push it up and down before twisting to remove it from the cap.

My Prep

Admittedly, living-cuisine recipes take preparation, and preparation takes time. But it's all about the approach. By getting a jump start on your weekly food prep, you'll be able to create healthy meals in just minutes throughout the week. I recommend reserving a specific time (usually two to four hours) on the same day each week to make items that can be easily refrigerated or stored in the pantry. I devote Sunday afternoons to stocking my shelves with ingredients I likely will need throughout the next seven days.

My weekly to-do list usually starts with a soup and a salad dressing (any recipes in this book work well for either), along with a dessert (try Moxie Bars, page 75) and two savory sauces. Basic Pesto (page 103) and Pumpkin Seed Cheese (page 171) are great flavor boosters for wraps, sandwiches, and pasta. I also dehydrate any bread, crackers, wraps, or tostada shells I might use. These items can be easily dried over-night, then removed in the morning and stored. Because grains are a weekly recipe staple in our home, I usually sprout 4 cups each of quinoa and buckwheat every week just to keep my grain bases covered. (Follow the directions in the previous section, making sure to refrigerate and rinse daily until you use them.)

My family also loves veggies for snacks and salads, so I try to cut and/or marinate a colorful mix each week. That may include 1 quart of cucumber sticks and/or 2 quarts each of julienned squash, shredded carrot, and diced tomatoes. I also chop 4 quarts of kale, sometimes combining and refrigerating the greens with walnuts and olives or raisins. I just need to add fresh dressing and maybe an avocado during my final prep. Every other week I add herb blends and granola to my tasks, just so I have a supply of each on hand.

There's no magic formula in terms of which foods you *should* prepare in advance. Just review your weekly menu for any staples that can be refrigerated or stored in the pantry. You'll be amazed by how a little planning and working ahead can ease your daily meal-prep stress. It can even make cooking a breeze.

A Final Note

Stocking your pantry with foods new to your palate can be intimidating, but think of it as just one step on the road to wellness. The good news with living cuisine is that you can experience healthy results by starting slow and building on ingredients you enjoy. Likewise, you don't need to retool your entire kitchen to be successful. If you have a blender, a cutting board, and a sharp knife, you're ready to get started. Still, as you start to experience great results, you might want to invest in a few new tools to streamline your prep time and preserve important nutrients. For a quick guide to my favorite kitchen things, take a peek at "Cook Like a Chef: A Guide to Quality Utensils," an appendix on page 251. You'll be suitably armed for Chapter 3, "Healing Basics: The Three-Day Jump Start." Let the healing begin!

HEALING BASICS: THE THREE-DAY JUMP START

The best way to begin a raw-foods diet is to jump right in! Even before you've finished stocking your pantry, you can start modifying your diet with a few simple recipes designed to put you on the path to good health.

"The Three-Day Jump Start" provides a dietary and lifestyle shift that will help you recalibrate and invigorate your systems with a blast of enzymes and other nutrients from vital plant-based items. You'll be experiencing the benefits of living foods almost immediately. The jump start draws from a variety of simple yet nutritious recipes that not only are quick to fix—five minutes or less—but also provide interesting mix-and-match options for your three-day menu.

How does it work? By enjoying healthy, vibrant, and anti-inflammatory living foods for just three days, you are alkalizing your body. Disease cannot live in an alkaline environment. You are putting your body back in balance—homeostasis—where it most wants to be! You are also supplying your body with the most nutrient-dense foods on the planet, which are also rich with water content, in a way it can easily absorb these nutrients: by using the enzymes available in the living foods to do all the work.

The jump start incorporates soups, salads, sauces, and other dishes I refer to as "separates" because they're stand-alone dishes that can be prepared in advance and incorporated however you wish. You can easily combine them with one another and with fresh produce for a meal or snack. For instance, not only is Pumpkin Seed Cheese (page 171) a fabulous filler for napa cabbage leaves, but by adding a cup of fresh vegetables (corn, shredded carrot, diced avocado, and chopped spinach) and topping the mixture with Avocado Citrus Dressing (page 143), you also have an awesome raw leaf taco. Likewise, Superfoods Yogurt (page 47) becomes an interesting parfait when dressed up with fresh blueberries and Creative Crunchy Granola (page 76).

Putting It into Practice: The Three-Day Jump Start

Although it's called "The Three-Day Jump Start," feel free to try this meal program for a week or even up to a month for a healthy lifestyle change. (You'll find the recipes in this chapter and throughout *Healing with Raw Foods*.) If you enjoy the benefits, don't be afraid to vary the menus by incorporating other recipes and playing with seasonal fresh fruits and vegetables, modifying the ingredients to keep the experience fresh and flavorful. The beauty of the menu is that creativity counts and also makes the process something to celebrate!

Three-Day Jump Start Meal-Planning Guide

The overall goal with these three days is to give the body a break from processed and refined foods and create an alkaline environment by pairing foods that cover necessary nutrition basics. This guide provides a balanced journey toward transitional eating. Each meal of the day has a few options to choose from. I've laid this menu out so that regardless of which meals you pick, you will still be enjoying balanced nutrition throughout your day. I've included below a few ways to look at each meal, to adjust your mind-set for success on this program. It's perfectly fine to enjoy one or more food preparations multiple times throughout the day (for instance, having the same snack in the morning and in the afternoon). As long as your overall day involves variety, you are moving forward in a powerful direction.

Breakfast: Breakfast powerfully sets up your day for success. By the numbers, you are 30 percent more likely to eat well throughout the day if you start the day off right, so here's to a healthy breakfast. You'll see a few smoothies listed here; these intentionally include your nutrition basics so that they can be considered a meal in a cup. You could pick one you love and run with it every day if you wish—that's what I do!

- Pomegranate Parfait (page 132)
- Balance Smoothie (page 43)
- Brainpower Smoothie (page 73)
- Superfoods Yogurt (page 47)

Midmorning Snack: Depending on your current routine, you may or may not need a midmorning snack. Several clients of mine who are very active report finding the midmorning snack to be an optimal way to boost energy and maintain stamina between breakfast and lunch, and in this way they are sure to avoid any food emergencies. You should consider this a smaller meal and one that includes healthy fats in order to stimulate the brain.

- Moxie Bar (page 75)
- Balanced Trail Mix (page 78)
- Superfoods Yogurt (page 47)

Lunch: Lunch should include at least 80 percent fresh fruits and vegetables, and it should be balanced with denser nuts, seeds, and sprouted grains in the form of a topping, sauce, or wrap. For this reason, I find most people have success enjoying entrée salads or squash pastas. To make it even easier, use these recipes as a guide for ingredients and toss together your favorite greens, toppings, and one of these simple dressings, and you are set for a health habit at lunchtime.

- Thai Lime Wrap (page 107)
- Greenie Salad with Spirit of Fire Soup (pages 48 and 238)
- Garden Gazpacho with Greenie Salad (pages 125 and 48)
- Fusion Pasta with side of Down South Greens (pages 221 and 110)
- Make your own salad

Midafternoon Snack: Afternoon snacks should provide clean-burning fuel and be a quick pick-me-up. Many of our desserts actually double as great afternoon snacks!

- Balanced Trail Mix (page 78)

- Superfoods Yogurt (page 47)

- Dulce de Leche Pineapple (page 201)

- Red Walnut and Date Snack (page 216)

Dinner: Dinner is a good time to round out your day with any missing pieces. For many of my clients, this is when they wind down, so they will put their heaviest meal at dinnertime. The important thing to remember about dinner is to enjoy it before 8 P.M. if possible. This will allow time for adequate digestion before bed.

- Rolled Squash Snack (page 147)

- Longevity Wrap (page 105)

- Fusion Pasta with side of Down South Greens (pages 221 and 110)

- Rolled Street Tacos (page 129)

Basics for Success

In addition to the Three-Day Jump Start, there are other simple things you can do to initiate a living-foods lifestyle. Each week, try enjoying just one of the following six easiest recipes in the book. These staple recipes are an indispensable part of my daily diet, and three of them form the basics of this Three-Day Jump Start. With a few basic ingredients, they provide a quick and easy way to add nutritious versatility to any menu. Use them for a meal, or look to them as snacks during the day. They make creating a wellness routine simple. I definitely recommend spending two to four hours in preparation for your success throughout the week—shopping and making some sauces, possibly preparing the vegetables for your plan in advance—which will save you even more time.

1 cup water

1 tablespoon almond
butter or other
nut butter, or 2
tablespoons hemp
seeds

1 tablespoon raw
sweetener of choice
(optional)

Makes one
8-ounce
serving

ALMOND SHORTCUT MILK

Quick and easy, this nutty milk substitute is a nutritious
accompaniment to any living-cuisine meal. Double the
recipe and share a glass.

1. Place all the ingredients in a blender and blend until
combined.

2. Pour into a glass and drink immediately.

BALANCE SMOOTHIE

With its blend of vitamins, minerals, proteins, and essential fatty acids, this smoothie contains all the ingredients for a quick, nutritious meal.

....

1. Place all the ingredients in a blender and blend until combined.

2. Pour into a glass and drink immediately.

1 cup Almond Shortcut Milk (page 42) or other nut milk

1 cup fresh berries, such as strawberries or blueberries

1 cup fresh spinach with stems

1 teaspoon raw honey or other natural sweetener

Makes one 16-ounce serving

1 cup fresh coconut or almond milk

1 banana

½ cup spinach

2 kale leaves

1 tablespoon blended greens powder like Dr. Schulze's SuperFood, Vitamineral Green, or spirulina

1 tablespoon raw agave nectar or 1 drop liquid stevia

Ice (optional)

Makes one 16-ounce serving

SUPERGREEN SMOOTHIE

Whether you're launching your raw-foods diet slowly, with sustained vigor, or through the power of a one-week detox, a Supergreen Smoothie delivers a quick shot of nutrients in an easy-to-digest-and-use format. Consisting of three base ingredients—fresh seasonal fruits, superfoods, and coconut milk or almond milk—this recipe yields an extra dose of greens minus the salad.

Mix all the ingredients in a blender and enjoy as a meal any time of day.

2 cups hot water*

1 teaspoon
 unpasteurized miso

1 teaspoon tahini paste

1 clove garlic (optional)

Makes
two 8-ounce
servings

BALANCE ME TONIC

Tahini paste and miso may be unfamiliar ingredients to your palate, but the nutty flavors give this tonic interest as well as nutrients. You may wish to add essential minerals, such as the Earth line from www.healthforce nutritionals.com.

Blend all the ingredients and enjoy immediately as a balancing, restorative tonic.

*In living-cuisine prep, 100° to 110°F constitutes "hot"; 80° to 100°F constitutes "lukewarm." Temperatures can be measured easily with a standard candy thermometer.

SUPERFOODS YOGURT

Delicious with fresh fruit or sprinkled with hemp seeds or raw cacao nibs, this yogurt is perfect for breakfast, lunch, or a midday snack.

1. Combine all the ingredients in a blender and blend until rich and creamy.

2. Refrigerate and enjoy within 3 days for optimal taste and texture.

1 Hass avocado, peeled, pitted, and chopped, or the flesh of 1 young Thai coconut, scooped from the coconut

1 cup coconut water

¼ cup supergreen powder

2 tablespoons fresh lemon juice

2 tablespoons raw honey or other natural sweetener

1 pinch sea salt

Makes one 8-ounce serving

2 tablespoons fresh lemon juice

1 tablespoon extra-virgin olive oil (for lighter taste) or flaxseed oil (for hearty, nutty taste)

2 cups fresh organic greens

½ Hass avocado, peeled and pitted

½ cup chopped cucumber

1 tablespoon dulse flakes

Makes
2 servings

GREENIE SALAD

Organic leafy greens are the focus of this side or stand-alone dish. I love red chard, green leaf lettuce, and red leaf lettuce combined together for this simple salad.

1. Whisk the lemon juice and olive oil together in a salad bowl.

2. Add the greens, avocado, cucumber, and dulse flakes.

3. Toss well and serve immediately.

Your Healing Path

Whichever recipes you prepare or steps you take in incorporating living foods into your diet, you'll be amazed by how quickly you'll gain energy, mental clarity, improved sleeping patterns, and even healthy, glowing skin. During this same time, you'll be giving your body a break from the negative diet-related habits that have been holding you back from good health, such as:

- Eating foods that aren't beneficial because they're heavily processed, contain additives, or are contaminated with pesticides and other growing agents

- Eating in a hurry, late at night, as a way to fill an emotional void, or without regard to how a food affects your body

- Microwaving or preparing foods in ways that destroy nutrient content

- Eating at restaurants that don't embody your value system regarding food

- Failing to balance your diet appropriately to ensure optimal nutrition

Initially, you may experience some general signs that your body is adjusting to a healthier inner terrain as you eliminate toxins and shift toward a more energetic field. You may be lethargic. You may suffer cravings and headaches along with greater or more frequent bowel eliminations. You may even have head cold–like symptoms as your body starts eliminating toxins via mucus. All this is completely natural. Be gentle on yourself. Embrace the process, knowing that you're giving your body time to heal. (As a mentor of mine has shared, "Better out than in!") It takes time for your brain to adjust to any new habit. Once you get over that initial hump, however, you'll find it easier to make better dietary choices. You may even wonder why it seemed so difficult at first!

Baby Steps for Starters

Rest assured, a raw-foods diet doesn't have to be an all-or-nothing proposition, especially in the beginning. You can ease into a living-foods way of life. And even if you don't become a complete "raw foodie," you can still experience positive results by making living-cuisine choices part of your daily diet. Because it's all about exploring possibilities, try it for a day, incorporate one meal a week, or just add one living food or ingredient to your eating plan to get comfortable with new tastes and textures. (A tablespoon of hemp seeds or dulse flakes in a salad, for instance, is a simple start.) Keep the ones you like and return to them.

As you gain confidence, you can explore and connect with other options. Of course, the higher the percentage of raw choices in your diet, the better the results! If you're hurting, concentrate on the parts of your body that are causing you the most suffering. By inventorying specific health areas and taking dietary action steps to improve them, you'll be on the path to healing. Perhaps, like me, your trouble involves digestive issues. Although every dish you eat must pass muster for your gastrointestinal (GI) tract, you may want to make this system your first target. Keep in mind, of course, that any positive change to your diet is a step forward.

In fact, "transitional foods" are a great way of integrating additional enzymes and nutrients into your menu even if you're not ready to move full speed into living cuisine. The term *transitional foods* generally refers to any fresh vegetable or other living food lightly cooked rather than served raw. But when you're just getting started, "transitional" can refer to your favorite produce, prepared at *higher* than 118°F. You just need to choose a cooking method—lightly steaming, baking, or parboiling—that creates minimal toxins in the process. If you can't let go of potatoes, for instance, steam or bake a yam and top it with dehydrated vegetables and a fresh raw tahini sauce for a dish that's still rich in living nutrition. If this balanced option is still too complicated, lightly steam your vegetables and drizzle them with raw oil instead of sautéing them in butter. By taking these shortcuts, or even making a few well-chosen swaps, you're increasing your nutrient intake while moving one step closer to a living-foods lifestyle. Even small transitional changes can lead to increased energy and digestive relief. Every little bit counts in motivating you to push forward!

When I began my journey to health and recovery, I wasn't fully committed to a raw-foods diet for the rest of my life. I was willing to try it for the time being, however, confident that I could always go back to my grilled steaks and baked potatoes. I had nothing to lose except, of course, my constant discomfort. Surprise, surprise. Within a week of eating 100 percent raw foods, I felt invigorated. Within no time, I no longer experienced the debilitating side effects of my abdominal disorders. Today I'm symptom-free, completely healed, and passionate about how different eating choices changed my life. In fact, as I progressed with my new choices, I also noticed that I was constantly refocusing on thoughts and actions that served my higher purpose, rather than the negative forces in my life. I finally felt free to be what I was meant to be, discovering how my improving health would fuel my future, not just personally but also professionally. I quickly moved from interest to commitment and then to passion based on my incredible results.

I recognize that not everyone experiences such startling results, at least not right away. Don't worry if you resort to old patterns along the way as you test the efficacy of this diet and lifestyle. The process can take time. Most of us, after all, are creatures of habit. Creating more positive habits can be a long journey. It may even involve a setback or two. Your body's reaction to detoxifying, for instance, can feel more like a health reversal than a move forward.

But like falling off a bike, just get back on and pedal forward. By concentrating on one day, one raw food, or one health solution at a time, you'll eventually feel the results of staying committed. You'll see the benefits and want to add to them!

A Final Note

"The Three-Day Jump Start" is only the beginning of an exciting transition from your old diet to your new lifestyle. In opening your mind to new possibilities, however, you've already made a critical commitment to your overall well-being. With every recipe you try, you're turning commitment into action and action into results. So how do you parlay your initial investment into a healthy lifestyle? By turning your attention next to Chapter 4, "Food as Preventive Medicine."

PART TWO

Healing

FROM HEAD TO TOE

CHAPTER 4

FOOD AS
PREVENTIVE MEDICINE

I believe there's no better form of preventive medicine than choosing fresh living foods. Eating is the one activity we all engage in several times a day *without fail*. What you put on your fork has a nutritional and healing impact not only for today but for the future as well. Many longevity experts agree, suggesting that diet and lifestyle can indeed influence your capacity for living a longer, high-quality life. A selection of groundbreaking studies targeting Seventh-Day Adventists over the past 50-plus years, for instance, champions the idea that lifestyle choices, especially involving a plant-based diet, can reduce the incidence of disease. More important, it may even increase longevity up to ten years.

Since 1960, Loma Linda (California) University School of Public Health researchers, in conjunction with the National Institutes of Health and other agencies, have focused on the fundamentalist Christian community because of its members' unique dietary habits. They abstain from animal products, sugar, alcohol, and caffeine while actively pursuing vegetarian, sometimes even vegan, diets. Also, besides avoiding cigarette smoking, Adventists are known for healthy lifestyle choices such as regular exercise and attention to both optimal body weight and body mass index.

Loma Linda scientists are exploring the precise links between those healthy choices and disease prevention via the

Adventist Health Study-2, a 2002-initiated research project involving more than 96,000 American and Canadian community members. Their current work builds on two previous studies that actually raised scientific awareness of the link between diet and healthy outcomes decades ago. In tracking 24,000 California members from 1960 to 1965, the Adventist Mortality Study demonstrated decreased death rates for some cancers as well as a lower incidence of heart disease.

During the Adventist Health Study-1, scientists tracking 34,000 participants between 1974 and 1988 were able to link specific eating habits (such as consuming legumes, nuts, and tomatoes) to a reduced incidence of certain cancers and heart disease. Both studies indicated longer life expectancies among Adventists over fellow Californians (up to 7.3 years in men and 4.4 years in women), with the second trial suggesting that a combination of lifestyle and dietary choices accounted for a life expectancy bonus of up to ten years. By including a broader pool of people, the latest Loma Linda project, Adventist Health Study-2, seeks to understand these links in greater detail. (For further information, see www.adventisthealth study.com.)

What scientific concept may explain why people enjoy such good health and even potential longevity? I believe that the chemical reaction of food in our bodies makes the difference. More specifically, two variables come into play: (1) The foods we consume are either *acidic* or *alkaline* by nature, and (2) they react in the body, creating either an *acidic* or an *alkaline* response. Put simply, each bite of food you consume shifts your body either into a corrosive acidic state—in which disease can set in—or into a balanced or alkaline state where disease is held at bay. If it sounds like chemistry, it is!

The Acid-Alkaline Connection

Let's take a closer look at what's really occurring with every item that you eat. Scientists measure the strength of acidity or alkalinity of both foods and the human body by pH, or potential of hydrogen, on a scale of 1 to 14, with 7 being neutral. Zero through 6 is considered acidic, while 8 to 14 is alkaline. Body fluids are designed, by nature, to be slightly alkaline at 7.4.

Many foods common to a standard American diet are acidic in nature, meaning they have the power to radically shift the body to the acidic end of the spectrum. Major offenders include meat, dairy, and other animal products as well as food additives and the preservatives that give shelf stability to packaged products. It's not just the food itself, but also how it's prepared. For instance, cooked olive oil produces a different pH than raw olive oil.

Whenever you consume a food that creates an acidic reaction in your body, you essentially launch an attack on yourself. Normal functioning is on hold while your cells, the basis of every vital system and organ, work feverishly to restore an alkaline state. For instance, eating fried food often causes indigestion and heartburn, an acidic reaction that creates stress on the digestive tract. Instead of appropriating vital nutrients, your body must work hard to alkalize this area first. This can lead to fatigue and other issues that aren't helpful to optimal digestion. When such emergencies occur on a daily basis, you're left exposed to "un-health" or "dis-ease."

But when your body is in an alkaline state, it's homeostatic, or balanced. Your cells go about their business, supporting your systems, delivering nutrients, and allocating resources for optimal function. In short, the body thrives. An alkaline state (or alkaline reaction) promotes production of important nerve signals called neurotransmitters—dopamine and serotonin are two well-known examples—in the brain. They play critical roles in stimulating many body functions, including our ability to feel good. Alkalinity means that your vital organs and functions are flourishing. Disease is inhibited because the chemistry doesn't support it. What's more, when your body is physically in balance, your mental and emotional well-being are, too. In other words, you're better able to understand, connect with, and take on the world. Because you feel good, you're in a more graceful and loving space.

So how do raw foods work to create such a state? Devoid of processing-related and other toxins but brimming in water content, plant-based foods, such as dark leafy greens, offer the ultimate alkaline option because *they're* so alkaline in nature. When you make daily food choices with pH levels on the alkaline end of the spectrum, you help shift your body into an alkaline state, which can protect you from disease. But what happens when you feel yourself slipping into acidic territory from that desired alkaline state? How can you tell that you're losing your dietary footing? The answer is *stress*. As it builds in your body, it will show up as indigestion; heartburn; or even a tightening of your neck, shoulders, and jaw.

One of the fastest ways to move toward alkalinity is with a living-cuisine staple: green juice. Juicing has a heralded place among many healthy lifestyle regimens. Because the fiber has been removed, green juice, in particular, is directly absorbed into the bloodstream, altering the body's pH while delivering an alkalizing blend of vitamins and minerals. Besides decreasing your immediate stress symptoms or any inflammation you may be experiencing, a daily dose of juice can help balance the intake of more acidic items, such as coffee, if you haven't yet removed them from your new diet.

Charting an Alkaline Path

When you understand the chemistry and physics at play, especially in terms of how food reacts at a basic level in your body, you'll be empowered to choose combinations that lead to greater vitality. But until you're more attuned to the nature of living foods, it can be helpful to rely on the chart "Alkalizing vs. Acidifying Foods," on pages 60 and 61, in making decisions. It's a quick reference for many standard dietary and raw-food choices. Simply add up your selections to see on which side of the acidic-alkaline scale you fall. Give yourself two extra-credit points for choosing organic foods because items doused with pesticides before harvesting are definitely more acidic. And because your thoughts and emotions also can shift your body to one side of the chart or the other, make sure you check where you are. Alkalinity aligns with positive emotions, including peace and joy.

As you can easily see as you start to work with this chart, each food choice you make can be a powerful way to shift your health. By simply adding fresh chopped basil as a garnish, you can help alkalize a meal, or by including a spinach salad you can shift a plate of food to a balanced meal. I grew up eating meat and potatoes, all acidic. No wonder I was so sick! However, if I had just swapped my potatoes for spinach, I may have experienced a different reaction to my whole meal. I often wonder whether I would have been able to prevent my illness had I had this information 15 years ago. This tool may be your first step in getting a handle on your own health.

One last note: If you're interested in a more visual approach to acidity versus alkalinity, I recommend purchasing pH strips at your local health food store as a way to further monitor your choices. With a simple swipe of your saliva from under your tongue, you'll get a quick visual of the concept and a direct reading of where you fall.

The Nutrient Punch!

When I talk about nutrients in *Healing with Raw Foods*, I'm referring to any chemical or compound necessary for your body to function and survive. Carbohydrates, fats, and proteins are classified as *macro*nutrients because you need them in large amounts for energy. As the main sources of calories in your diet, they help your body carry out every possible metabolic process. (They're also why you're jazzed enough to take on every mental and physical activity of the day!) Although vitamins and minerals are necessary for metabolic and other functions, too, you need them in smaller, or *micro*nutrient, amounts.

Here's what more you should know about these nutrient powerhouses.

Carbohydrates

Foods that contain carbohydrates raise your blood sugar, or glucose, the universal energy source for each cell. Carbohydrates are classified as simple or complex, depending on their chemical structure and what they actually do in your body.

— **Simple carbohydrates.** These are basic sugars found in both natural and manufactured foods. In a plant-based diet, simple carbohydrates such as fructose (from fruit) and maltose (from vegetables) give your body a quick energy boost. In processed foods, however, they can also add empty sugar calories. By removing table sugar, white flour, low-calorie sweeteners, alcohols, "enriched" grains, and other standard American diet staples from your menu, you're also removing those hazards in favor of simple carbohydrates from fruit and vegetable sources.

— **Complex carbohydrates.** These energy sources are so named for their complicated structure. They're composed of both starches and dietary fiber. Digested slowly, starches provide sustained energy. They stay with you longer so you're energized and not tempted to nosh! Legumes (beans, lentils, and dried peas), starchy vegetables, and whole-grain products are great sources. (The term *whole grain* simply means that nutrients from every part of the grain—the center, the shell, and the middle layer—are accessible. Nothing has been refined away.)

— **Dietary fiber.** The fibrous, or indigestible, part of plant-based foods, fiber can make you feel full after eating, which can lead to weight loss, and is instrumental in keeping your digestive system functioning. Dietary fiber has also been implicated in reducing cholesterol levels and even your risk of heart disease and stroke. Beans and legumes, nuts, whole grains, fruits, and vegetables are great living-cuisine sources.

ALKALIZING VS.

Category	+4 Most Alkalizing	+3 More Alkalizing	+2 Alkalizing	+1 Least Alkalizing
Herbs	Cloves, Cinnamon, Oregano, Basil, Turmeric, Parsley, Ginseng	Thyme, Cumin	Green Tea, Ginger, Peppermint, Spearmint, Marjoram	Curry, Sage, Licorice Root, Burdock Root
Fruits*	Avocados, Persimmons, Papayas, Lemons, Limes, Blueberries	Plums, Blackberries, Oranges, Tangelos, Mangos, Grapes with Seeds	Apples, Pears, Pineapple, Raspberries, Strawberries, Peaches, Kiwi	Apricots, Nectarines, Honeydew, Cantaloupe, Bananas, Currants, Cherries, Cooked Tomatoes, Watermelon
Vegetables* & Legumes	Spinach, Kale, Collards, Swiss Chard, Dark Greens, Broccoli, Arugula, Nori, Wakame, Kombu, Hijiki	Cucumbers, Zucchini, Parsnips, Green Leaf Lettuce, Romaine Lettuce, Brussels Sprouts, Bok Choy	Sweet Potatoes, Beets, Cauliflower, Carrots, Bell Peppers, Pumpkin, Squash, Garlic, Onions	Soybeans, Tofu, Jicama, Celery, Green Peas, Asparagus, Adzuki Beans, Black Beans, Kidney Beans, Green Beans, Hummus
Grains, Cereals, Grasses & Soups	Wheatgrass, Chlorella, Spirulina, Blue-Green Algae, Miso Soup		Oats, Sumac, Sorghum, Lentils	Quinoa, Millet, Amaranth
Sprouts, Nuts & Seeds	Sprouts		Almonds, Pistachios, Hazelnuts	
Oils		Cod-Liver Oil	Evening Primrose Oil, Borage Oil, Cold-Pressed Extra-Virgin Olive Oil, Flaxseed Oil	
Meat, Fowl, Wild Game & Shellfish				Perhaps Sushi, If Wild-Caught
Dairy & Alternative Milks		Breast Milk		Coconut Milk, Rice Milk, Soy Milk
Beverages	Herbal Organic Teas, Bicarbonate	High-Quality Waters, Mineral Water		Filtered Water, Honey Wine, Red Wine
Sweeteners & Seasonings	Sea Salt		Blackstrap Molasses, Apple Cider Vinegar, Umeboshi, Stevia	

ACIDIFYING FOODS

Category	-1 Least Acidifying	-2 Acidifying	-3 More Acidifying	-4 Most Acidifying
Herbs				
Fruits*		Cranberries, Raw Tomatoes	Canned Fruit, Shelf Juices with Sugar or Corn Syrup	All Nonorganic Fruit
Vegetables* & Legumes	Potatoes, String Beans, Chickpeas	White Beans, Navy Beans, Pinto Beans	Processed Soy Products	
Grains, Cereals, Grasses & Soups	Brown Rice, Kasha, Teff	Buckwheat, Wheat, Semolina, Farina, Spelt	Maize, Corn, Rye, Barley, White Rice	White Bread
Sprouts, Nuts & Seeds	Peanuts, Pine Nuts, Sunflower Seeds			
Oils	Sesame Oil, Grapeseed Oil, Sunflower Oil, Almond Oil, Peanut Oil			Fried Foods, Trans-Fatty Acids, Partially Hydrogenated Oils, Vegetable Shortening
Meat, Fowl, Wild Game & Shellfish	All Organic Free-Range Meat & Eggs, Pacific Wild-Caught Fish	Goat, Lamb, Goose, Turkey, Shrimp, Duck, Venison	Chicken, Beef, Eggs, Crab, Scallops	Pork, Oysters, Lobsters, Catfish, Atlantic/ Farmed Fish
Dairy & Alternative Milks	Goat & Sheep's Milk Cheeses, Yogurt, Goat's Milk Products	Aged Cheeses, Organic Dairy Products		Cow's Milk, Cow's Milk Cheeses, Ice Cream
Beverages	Sake	Commercially Processed Black Tea		Soda, Diet Soda, Alcoholic Beverages
Sweeteners & Seasonings	Processed Honey, Raw Sugar, Brown Sugar	Vanilla Extract		NutraSweet, Equal, Sweet'N Low, Splenda, High-Fructose Corn Syrup

*Pesticides are acidic in nature, and fruits in particular, as well as other heavily sprayed crops like greens and root vegetables, will be affected by growing and spraying practices, making the food itself acidic. If buying conventional produce, be sure to soak and clean it well before consuming.

Because carbohydrates provide energy and protect against disease, the federal government's 2010 Dietary Guidelines for Americans recommends that they make up 45 to 65 percent of your daily caloric intake. But you need to choose wisely. Although simple carbohydrates provide energy, the bulk of your diet still needs to be complex carbohydrates because of their nutrient density. They deliver many benefits.

Protein/Amino Acids

Protein is critical for building and repairing cells, especially those of the bones, muscles, and skin. Insufficient supplies can cause serious health problems. Because a raw plant-based diet doesn't include meat, poultry, eggs, and seafood—common sources for all the essential amino acids necessary to manufacture complete proteins in the body—you'll need to supplement with a balanced variety of greens, beans, gluten-free grains, peas, nuts, and seeds.

The good news is that incorporating a variety of other foods into your meal plan can deliver enough amino acids to produce your daily protein requirement. Plant-based foods have the value-added nutrient effects of B vitamins (such as niacin, thiamin, riboflavin, and B_6), essential fatty acids, iron, zinc, and magnesium without the calories or saturated fat found in meat. By consuming a variety of selections throughout the day, you're not only improving your nutrient intake but also raising the associated potential health benefits.

Fats and Fatty Acids

Dietary fat supplies your body with energy, and essential fatty acids (omega-3 and omega-6) are necessary for proper growth, development, and overall health. They also aid in the absorption of the fat-soluble vitamins: A, D, E, and K. But not all fats are created equal. Fortunately, by choosing a raw-foods diet, you're automatically eliminating many foods that are rich in either cholesterol or saturated fats (from dairy products and meat) and trans fats (from processed foods), both of which are bad for your body. Instead, plant-based foods—nuts, seeds, and oils—yield one or both of the potentially healthy fats:

—**Monounsaturated fats.** These have been shown to improve blood cholesterol levels and may even help in controlling blood insulin, or sugar, levels. Olive oil, one of the richest monounsaturated sources, has been regularly linked to lower levels of "bad" and higher levels of "good" cholesterol.

— **Polyunsaturated fats (including essential fatty acids).** A key component in blood and oxygen circulation, omega-3 fatty acids positively affect blood cholesterol levels while decreasing the risk of heart disease and even type 2 diabetes. Omega-6 fatty acids aid in metabolism plus the promotion of healthy bones, skin, and hair. Essential fatty acids are found in soybeans, nuts, and various seeds as well as their extracted oils. Despite these sources, however, you may need supplements to meet your daily needs.

Micronutrients

Vitamins and minerals play vital roles in both growth and metabolism. They're considered micronutrients because your body requires relatively small quantities of them to do their essential work. Minerals are a mixed bag. Calcium, for instance, is so important to various functions that it's considered a macromineral. You need it in larger amounts than zinc or other trace minerals, which have something to contribute but in very small doses.

Apart from vitamin K, which is primarily formed via intestinal bacteria, and vitamin D, which is converted in the skin by sunlight, the remaining vitamins and minerals come from food. Vitamins are considered organic substances because they originate in living sources such as plants. Minerals are inorganic because they're present in the soil and leached through plants or other living sources on their way to your table.

Fortunately, the same fruits, vegetables, whole grains, nuts, and seeds that supply other nutrients are loaded with specific vitamins—A, C, E, the B complex, and folic acid—along with minerals of every sort.

Balancing Your Choices

A balanced diet is as important in living cuisine as it is with a traditional Western diet. Why? By ensuring that your daily menu includes variety both within and among various food groups, you're better able to meet recommended daily allowances (or values) for carbohydrates, proteins, fats, vitamins, and minerals.

Balanced food choices are particularly important with living cuisine because your food groups don't include traditional meat and dairy, which are natural sources of protein; vitamins A, B, and D; and calcium. Instead, your focus is on vegetables, fruits, whole grains, nuts, legumes, and beans, which provide varying amounts of those nutrients. Also, no single food can give you everything your body needs to function. Likewise, not all foods in a single group will yield the same nutrients. An orange may be high in vitamin C, for instance, but lacking in vitamin A, which you can get from cantaloupe. Thankfully, many plant-based foods provide multiple nutrients. For instance:

- *From grains:* Carbohydrates, fiber, proteins/amino acids, and some vitamins and minerals

- *From vegetables:* Vitamins A and C, folate, iron, magnesium, and other trace minerals

- *From fruits:* Vitamins A and C, potassium, and fiber

- *From legumes and nuts/seeds:* Amino acids/protein, B vitamins, iron, zinc, and essential fatty acids

Even though you'll need to individualize your eating plan, just keep proportions in mind. Because whole grains, vegetables, and fruits are important sources of macronutrients, you'll want to include more of them in your diet than other foods so you're covering your energy needs. With a raw-foods diet, you can eat right and be raring to go!

Harmony in All Things

Making daily choices that support the vital processes of your body in creating balanced, holistic well-being is at the heart of living cuisine. When you look upon food as having the power to heal, you'll understand how the items you select for breakfast or the menu you pick for lunch can affect whether or not your cold clears or your arthritis flares. The important point to remember about this diet is that different areas of your body will respond to specific nutrients and healing protocols, based on their function. So although it's important to think balance, you also want to focus on any health struggle or challenging area of the body.

Although food as a healing force is a topic of much debate in health care, some physicians and other practitioners readily recognize the body's incredible ability to heal with a diet focused entirely on plant-based foods. I've included some of their comments in this book along with simple recipes to get you started and additional nutritional resources to help you take the next step. Together, they should fuel your vision for achieving better health.

But there's another important ingredient to a living-cuisine lifestyle. When I began to uncover how the body functions and responds both positively and negatively to the chemical reactions triggered by what I eat, I was suddenly feeling great. I learned, however, that it's important not to get overwhelmed by the nuances of a raw-foods lifestyle, especially because new information is emerging at rapid-fire rates in this area of wellness. Details count, but you can spur healing even if you focus only on making food choices within general guidelines. In other words, don't sweat the small stuff.

I engaged others who would support me on this path. I encourage you to seek out integrative health practitioners who can partner with you and monitor your progress. You want someone on your team who embodies your value system in terms of eating and wellness, especially because your new dietary choices will be decidedly different from those of your neighbors. But then again, so will your outcome. Even though others may not understand your enthusiasm for aligning food with optimal health, rest assured that when the new you emerges, they'll want to know what you're doing! In fact, I encourage sharing your delicious new dishes with your skeptics at the same time you shower them with grace and love. Your friends, family members, and acquaintances will experience your joy and may even be inspired by your journey.

A Final Note

The preventive power of living cuisine is that it keeps your body—from your physical structure to your mental and emotional well-being—in balance. Avoiding heavily processed foods in favor of plant-based items can help create an alkaline environment that fosters health rather than triggers disease. But what does that mean for each system of the body? Scientists have yet to understand all the ramifications of a raw or living-foods diet because studies on the nutrient value of plant-based foods have commonly focused on solely vegetarian and vegan eating patterns. Yet evidence still suggests that the selections in this dietary approach can provide important nutrients to keep all parts of the body humming. (That's absolutely been my experience!) In Chapter 5, we explore their primary role in "Boosting Your Brain Health."

Advice from the Chef

To be forearmed:

- Stay ahead of the health game by enjoying superfoods throughout the week. Add goji berries or hemp seeds to everyday meals to support your body.

- Keep your nutritional needs in mind. When preparing your weekly menu, think in terms of high-protein sources, mineral-dense items, and other foods that support your health.

- Incorporate a range of foods into your daily diet. Because balance is achieved with various nutrients, make food variety the spice of life to ensure healthy results. A good rule of thumb is to eat according to the rainbow, integrating as many colorful choices as you can. Also follow the 80/20 rule of raw eating—80 percent fresh, 20 percent concentrated superfoods and "nutrient all-stars" such as nuts and seeds.

- Combine dishes to add an extra nutrient wallop. A Moxie Bar (page 75) paired with a glass of Warrior Mylk (page 157) is the best of all worlds!

- Use juicing and blended smoothies liberally. Full of nutrients, drinks such as the Family Five Smoothie (page 213) are a great first preventive step.

CHAPTER 5

BOOSTING YOUR BRAIN HEALTH

Can what you eat impact your brain's ability to fire on all cylinders? Research has repeatedly shown that diet can lead to obesity, which can result in heart disease, diabetes, hypertension, and even cancer. But now we know from extensive work by scientists that food choices can also affect the brain's capacity to function cognitively and regulate all aspects of your health.

The reason? You're not feeding it what it needs or in balanced proportions to function properly or support your overall health. Typical North American diet items are actually brain-unfriendly. Alcohol, for instance, kills off cells directly, while artery-clogging foods, such as animal meats and dairy products and other high-fat selections, can restrict essential blood flow. And high-glycemic-index foods in the forms of refined sugar and other starchy or processed items stimulate unhealthy, roller-coaster fluctuations in blood sugar. By breaking down too quickly in the body, these foods can produce many negative effects, including imbalances of dopamine, serotonin, and other important neurotransmitters.

When your body chemistry is out of whack, so is everything about how you think, feel, and act. Insufficient neurotransmitter levels, for instance, can lead to chronic fatigue, unhappiness, or depression. Moreover, research has demonstrated a link between obesity and declining brain function and mental acuity. Through his functional brain scans of National Football League players, Daniel G. Amen, M.D., renowned brain health expert, tied excessive weight and reduced blood flow to decreased attention, reasoning, and judgment. On the upside, his team also established that weight loss, exercise, and proper diet could yield vast improvements in brain health, especially memory and mood. "We've demonstrated that even if you have been bad to your brain," says Dr. Amen, "on the right program you can often reverse the damage and improve your life."

Brain-Saving Choices

The good news is that plant-based foods provide the essential high-quality fats, proteins/amino acids, vitamins, and minerals that your brain, like any organ, needs to function optimally. Besides being rich in nutrients and devoid of unhealthy fats or damaging chemicals, these choices are low in calories. That means they naturally regulate and support a favorable weight, which ultimately boosts brainpower. But which living-cuisine selections offer brain-boosting nutrients? The general answer is that many foods common to a raw diet provide chemistry-positive nutrients.

Blueberries, dark leafy greens, broccoli, and avocados are dense in essential phytonutrients that feed your brain in small caloric packages. They also provide the enzymes necessary for efficient digestion. Because the brain utilizes only 25 percent of calories consumed, enzymes are critical in getting the most from those sources.

Apples, melons, and apricots along with broccoli, mushrooms, and spinach offer low-glycemic complex carbohydrates. By slowly breaking down into simple sugars, they trigger a steady stream of energy rather than a surge followed by a plunge. That's important for maintaining balanced neurotransmitter levels. Other complex carbohydrates can be found in a variety of nuts, seeds, and whole grains.

Nuts, seeds, cacao, maca root, green tea, avocados, and leafy green vegetables are great sources for nonanimal protein and omega-3 fatty acids. "Good" or "healthy" omega-3 fatty acids keep blood vessels in your brain free of blockages while balancing sugar and dopamine levels and stimulating serotonin production. A diet replete in omega-3 fatty acids can ward off depression. It can be a positive mood-changer. In short, your brain needs fat to function!

Advice from the Chef

To boost your brain:

- Add a superingredient like E3Live to coconut yogurt in the morning. This intense green will help stimulate focus and turbocharge your brain.

- Incorporate superfood treats such as Moxie Bars (page 75) into your daily menu. These little squares will help power you mentally through the day.

- Use grains sparingly. When choosing them, gravitate to options such as quinoa, which is technically a seed, to maximize the whole-grain nutritional value.

- Put raw cacao in your next smoothie. Use it to help unleash your creativity and feel-good emotions.

- Keep your brain in mind by choosing healthy fats that fuel development and optimal functioning.

- Enjoy green smoothies instead of juice. By replacing a banana with greens and avocado, you'll get the additional fat and chlorophyll necessary to power your brain while slowing down the sugar effects of other fruit.

AFFIRMATIONS
for Brain Health

Author Louise Hay put it best when she wrote: "The glass is both half-full and half-empty depending on how you choose to look at it. There are literally billions of thoughts you can choose to think." My challenge: Select the thoughts that move you forward. Use positive affirmations to bolster your new dietary path, and change—for the better—the way you perceive, deal with, or take on life.

- *To counter anxiety:* "I love and approve of myself. I trust the process of life. I am safe."

- *To stay on track with your diet:* "Eating new, enriching foods is good for my mental well-being."

BRAINPOWER SMOOTHIE

Smoothies offer a refreshing dose of nutrition in the morning or afternoon. Try this one to boost concentration.

....

1. Combine all the ingredients in a blender and blend well until creamy.

2. Pour into a glass and drink immediately.

1 cup blueberries

1 cup coconut water (or regular water)

½ Hass avocado, peeled and pitted

¼ cup yacon syrup or 3 drops liquid stevia

2 tablespoons maca root

½ cup ice (optional)

Makes 16 ounces for 1 or 2 servings

1 cup Almond Shortcut Milk (page 42) or hemp milk

1 medium to large banana

2 tablespoons raw cacao nibs (optional)

1 tablespoon spirulina

1 tablespoon coconut butter or almond butter

1 teaspoon ground cinnamon

1 to 3 drops liquid stevia

½ cup ice (optional)

Makes one 16-ounce shake

SPIRULINA SHAKE

A tablespoon of spirulina in your morning smoothie provides brain-nourishing essential amino acids and protein to stimulate clarity and better concentration.

1. Place the almond milk, banana, cacao nibs, and spirulina in the blender. Blend until combined.

2. Add the coconut butter, cinnamon, stevia, and ice. Blend for 20 seconds, until smooth and creamy.

3. Pour into a glass and drink immediately.

MOXIE BARS

These healthy bars packing brain-nourishing berries and nuts can be enjoyed as an afternoon snack or a breakfast bar.

....

1. Place the walnuts in a food processor and process until finely ground, like the consistency of nut meal. Add the coconut shreds, yacon syrup, Warrior Food, and salt and process until the ingredients come together to form a dough.

2. Remove the dough and press evenly into a 6 × 6-inch (or an 8 × 8-inch) glass dish.

3. Place the blueberries in the food processor and pulse until chopped. Do not puree. Spread the berries evenly over the crust.

4. Cover and refrigerate the bars until ready to enjoy. (They can also be enjoyed immediately!)

Note: Moxie Bars keep for up to a week in the refrigerator.

2 cups walnuts

½ cup coconut shreds

¼ cup yacon syrup or 3 drops liquid stevia

2 tablespoons Warrior Food or other plant-based protein supplement

1 teaspoon sea salt

2 cups blueberries

Makes nine 2 × 2-inch bars

2 cups blueberries or raisins

2 cups walnut butter or almond butter

2 cups hulled buckwheat groats, soaked and drained

1 cup coconut shreds

½ cup sliced almonds

¼ cup yacon syrup or 3 drops liquid stevia

2 tablespoons plant-based protein supplement (optional)

1 tablespoon ground cinnamon

1 teaspoon sea salt

Makes
7 cups

CREATIVE CRUNCHY GRANOLA

Enjoy this delicious granola for breakfast or by the handful on the run. With 12 grams of protein per ¼-cup serving, it's a great way to stimulate energy and keep you focused, especially midday.

1. In a large bowl using a spatula, combine all the ingredients.

2. Line a dehydrator tray with your choice of a nonstick surface. Using a spatula, spread the granola onto the sheet no more than ½ inch deep.*

3. Place the tray in the dehydrator. Set the dehydrator at 115°F. Dehydrate the granola until completely dry and crunchy. Generally it takes about 12 hours, but because granola can never be too dry or crunchy, don't be afraid to extend the drying time for another 2 to 4 hours. It won't hurt the final product. Rotate the tray halfway through the drying process for even dehydration, however.

*Although this recipe fills one 15¼ × 13-inch tray of a square Sedona nine-tray dehydrator, tray sizes vary with each appliance, so you may have to adjust. Just make sure the granola is no more than ½ inch deep.

Note: Store the granola in a covered container in the refrigerator for up to 2 weeks.

2 cups shelled pumpkin
   seeds

2 cups goji berries

1 cup hemp seeds

1 cup dried mulberries

1 cup raw cacao nibs
   (optional)*

Makes
seven
1-cup
servings

BALANCED TRAIL MIX

To truly support optimal health, this trail mix combines
a balanced selection of essential fatty acids and antioxidants in a blend of tasty ingredients. Enjoy as a snack or
an addition to cereals, parfaits, and fruit salads.

Toss together and hit the trail!

*I recommend adding the cacao nibs only if you enjoy the bitter
flavor. This mix lasts indefinitely, so you can easily double or triple
the contents to family-size it.

CHERRY TOMATO TAPAS

This lively tapas plate is just as functional as it is fun! For this dish, cherry tomatoes are tossed with memory-enhancing herbs and topped with a brain-boosting marinade.

....

1. To make the tomatoes, in a medium-size mixing bowl, combine the cherry tomatoes, cilantro, hemp seeds, and avocado and toss together. Let the mixture sit while preparing the marinade.

2. To make the marinade, in a blender process the red bell pepper, almond milk, olive oil, curry powder, raw honey, sea salt, and garlic until a medium-bodied marinade is achieved.

3. In a medium-size mixing bowl, toss the tomato mixture in the marinade until well coated. Garnish with a sprinkle of sea salt and serve.

Note: The tapas can be stored in an airtight container in the refrigerator for up to 3 days.

For the tomatoes:
6 cups cherry tomatoes, sliced in half lengthwise

½ cup finely chopped cilantro leaves

½ cup hemp seeds

1 Hass avocado, peeled, pitted, and diced

For the marinade:
1 red bell pepper, stem and seeds removed

¼ cup Almond Shortcut Milk (page 42) or coconut milk

2 tablespoons extra-virgin olive oil or flaxseed oil

1 tablespoon yellow curry powder

1 tablespoon raw honey or 1 date

1 teaspoon sea salt

1 clove garlic

Makes 6 appetizer servings

2 cups diced zucchini

1 cup ground golden flaxseeds

4 cups water

2 tablespoons desired seasoning*

Makes about twelve ⅛-inch-thick wraps

BASIC FLAX WRAPS

Simple and fast, these wraps are a nutrient-filled addition to any meal. Make them in advance and refrigerate until you're ready to form a healthy raw-food sandwich.

1. In a blender combine the zucchini, ground golden flaxseeds, and water (in that order for best results). Blend well until thick and creamy. Add the desired seasoning and blend again.

2. Line 3 dehydrator trays with nonstick drying sheets. Carefully spread the mixture over the sheets ⅛ inch thick.

3. Place the sheets in the dehydrator and dehydrate at 118°F for 5 to 6 hours. To shorten the drying time, flip the wrap over after 4 hours. (The wrap may shrink from the edges of the sheet.)

4. Cut each sheet into 4 equal segments and store in the refrigerator.

*Use your imagination or try one of the spice blends under "Mixing It Up" on page 23.

Note: Basic Flax Wraps can be stored in an airtight container in the refrigerator for up to 2 weeks.

AVOCADO "OMEGA" WRAP

Dr. Amen refers to avocado as "God's butter," and I would have to agree! By providing omega-3 and omega-6 fatty acids, the avocado and hemp butter in this recipe are nutrient chargers that make this choice a great substitute for fish. Sprinkle with Italian Blend (page 23) for a delicious entrée that can be made in advance. It's nutrition on the go!

1. Lay the wrap out flat on a cutting board. Spread the hemp butter over three-fourths of the wrap, working your way across horizontally.

2. Arrange the avocado slices on top of the hemp butter, followed by the spinach, cucumber, and carrots. Sprinkle with sea salt.

3. Tightly roll up the wrap. Slice the wrap in half lengthwise diagonally.

4. Serve accompanied with the Curry Marinade.

1 Flax Wrap (page 80) or 1 raw nori piece (approximately 8 × 6½ inches)

2 tablespoons hemp butter

½ Hass avocado, peeled, pitted, and sliced lengthwise

1 cup chopped spinach leaves

¼ cup julienned cucumber

¼ cup shredded carrot or beet

Sea salt, to taste

¼ cup Curry Marinade (page 85), for dipping

Makes 1 entrée or 2 appetizer servings

QUINOA TABBOULEH

A gluten-free, protein-rich grain, quinoa makes this tabbouleh-type salad special. Whether raw sprouted or lightly steamed, quinoa is rich in nutrients and nutty, creamy, crunchy flavor.

....

1. Place the tahini, lemon juice, cilantro, scallion, garlic powder, and sea salt in a food processor. Blend until smooth.

2. Transfer the tahini dressing to a mixing bowl and add the quinoa. Using a spatula, fold the ingredients together to combine.

3. For additional flavor, add chopped serrano peppers or sun-dried tomatoes to taste.

4. Serve immediately or refrigerate so the flavors can meld.

*To sprout raw quinoa, cover the quinoa with water and soak for 8 to 12 hours at room temperature. (You'll see tiny tails on the grains.) Rinse and then use. To steam, place the quinoa in a steamer basket over a pot of water on the stove and steam for 7 minutes if presoaked and 15 minutes if not.

Note: With the inclusion of lemon juice as a natural preservative, this dish can be stored in the refrigerator for up to a week.

1½ cups tahini

½ cup fresh lemon juice

¼ cup chopped cilantro leaves

¼ cup chopped scallion

1 teaspoon garlic powder

1 teaspoon sea salt

6 cups quinoa, sprouted or steamed*

Serrano peppers or sun-dried tomatoes, chopped, to taste (optional)

Makes 6 cups

4 cups (about 12 ounces) Asian broccoli, sliced lengthwise

½ cup walnuts, chopped

1 recipe Curry Marinade (page 85)

Makes four 1-cup servings

CURRY-MARINATED ASIAN BROCCOLI

Long, skinny, and soft, Asian broccoli adds a different texture to this vegetable dish. Used for lunch or saved for dinner, this dish can also be made with regular broccoli or broccolini. In any case, it's a sweet and satisfying nutrient-dense main course.

1. Add the broccoli and walnuts to the marinade and toss well to coat.

2. Allow the mixture to sit for 1 hour in the refrigerator for softer broccoli or dehydrate the mixture for 2 hours at 115°F for an intensified flavor.

Note: The broccoli can be stored in an airtight container in the refrigerator for up to 4 days.

CURRY MARINADE

A sweet and savory sauce that can be used for marinating or dipping, Curry Marinade plays many roles in a raw-foods diet. Don't let the word *marinade* fool you, though. This coconut butter–based liquid is great for flavoring vegetables and fabulous as a condiment.

1. Combine all the ingredients in a blender.

2. Blend until smooth and emulsified with no large pieces of garlic.

3. Pour the marinade into an appropriate bowl for mixing or dipping.

2 tablespoons coconut butter

1 small clove garlic

2 tablespoons yellow mild curry powder

2 drops liquid stevia

1 teaspoon sea salt

Makes about 2 tablespoons

2 tomatoes (heirloom, beefsteak, or any other tomato that you enjoy)

For the filling:
1 cup spinach leaves

½ cup basil leaves

½ cup extra-virgin olive oil

1 teaspoon sea salt

4 cloves garlic

⅓ cup pistachios

1 Hass avocado, peeled, pitted, and diced

4 cups diced mixed vegetables, such as summer squash, red chard, and red bell pepper

Makes 2 entrée or 4 appetizer servings

TOMATO STACKS WITH SPINACH PESTO FILLING

This dish spotlights one of nature's nutrient workhorses —the tomato. Rich in lycopene, a powerful antioxidant known for its cancer-protective properties, these garden fruits are tasty and versatile. Although any tomato works in this dish, try heirloom varieties. Produced from seeds passed down through the generations, they're prized for their flavor and color diversity.

1. Horizontally slice the tomatoes into ⅓-inch-thick rounds. (Coring is optional.) Set aside.

2. To make the filling, blend the spinach, basil leaves, olive oil, sea salt, and garlic in a blender until pureed.

3. Add the pistachios and blend again until a thick mixture or pesto of coarse or fine particles has formed.

4. Place the avocado and diced vegetables in a bowl. Add the pesto and toss well to coat the vegetables.

5. On a cutting board, layer one slice of tomato, followed by ¼ cup of the mixture. Repeat twice to create an upright stack.

Note: This dish is best enjoyed immediately, but the filling can be made ahead and refrigerated. Assemble the dish just before serving.

For the filling:

2 cups shredded carrot

2 cups chopped cauliflower

½ cup chopped spinach

2 tablespoons extra-virgin olive oil

1 cup macadamia nuts, pine nuts, or almonds

1½ cups water

¼ cup ground golden flaxseeds

1 tablespoon turmeric

1 teaspoon sea salt

1 clove garlic

1 scallion

For the crust:

1 cup walnuts or pecans

½ cup carrot juice (can use water or apple juice if no carrot juice is available)

2 tablespoons Italian Blend (page 23)

1 teaspoon sea salt

VEGETABLE QUICHE

Similar in body to the traditional egg quiche, this dish fits beautifully into a raw-foods dietary plan because of its high nutrient content. A variety of vegetables come together in a tasty dish that can be served for lunch or dinner.

1. To make the filling, in a large mixing bowl, toss together the carrots, cauliflower, spinach, and olive oil. Let the mixture sit while preparing the other ingredients.

2. In a blender combine the macadamia nuts, water, flaxseeds, turmeric, sea salt, garlic, and scallion. Blend until well combined and thick.

3. To make the crust, in a food processor fitted with the S-blade, add the walnuts and pulse until broken down into a fine meal. Add the carrot juice, Italian Blend spices, and sea salt. Process until a dough-like mixture has formed. Remove the mixture and pat into an 8-inch round glass dish or 6 individual quiche molds.

4. Toss together the vegetable mixture and the macadamia mixture, folding together until well combined.

5. Top the quiche crust evenly with the vegetable mixture.

6. Enjoy the quiche fresh or dehydrate. By removing the moisture, dehydrating sharpens the flavor and produces a traditional quiche-like texture. Set at 118°F for 2 hours.

Note: The quiche can be stored in the refrigerator for up to 3 days.

Makes 6 servings

BLUEBERRY NO-BAKE COCONUT COOKIES

Who thinks of cookies for the brain? (I do!) These are a delicious way to rev your mind and body, whether they're a snack for breakfast or a dessert to top off any other meal. With an extra kick of ginger, they're a fun way to spice up your meal plan.

1. In a food processor fitted with the S-blade, process the dates into a paste.

2. Add the coconut butter, followed by the coconut flour, sea salt, and coconut flakes. Process into a dough-like mixture.

3. Add the maca root and hemp seeds; pulse.

4. Add the blueberries and pulse again briefly.

5. Scoop out 2-inch balls and place into paper candy cups.

6. Refrigerate and enjoy throughout the week as a breakfast snack or dessert.

⅔ cup dates

2 tablespoons coconut butter

1 cup coconut flour

1 teaspoon sea salt

2 cups coconut flakes or raw desiccated coconut

2 tablespoons maca root

⅓ cup hemp seeds

16 ounces blueberries

Makes
12 cookies

WALNUT BUTTER DESSERT BARS

Like other desserts, these bars can double as snacks or even breakfast options. Fresh walnuts in the butter add protein and flavor.

....

1. To make the walnut butter, in a food processor fitted with the S-blade, process the walnuts, sea salt, and stevia until rich and creamy, scraping down the sides as necessary. Set aside.

2. To make the dough, pulse the steel-cut oats, cinnamon, and ginger mixture until a dry dough has formed.

3. Fold the walnut butter into the dry dough until combined, and press the mixture into an 8 × 8-inch glass baking dish. Garnish the bars with banana flakes or top with fresh fruit as you enjoy each bar.

For the walnut butter:
2 cups walnuts

Pinch of sea salt

1 drop liquid stevia

For the dough:
2 cups steel-cut oats or raw buckwheat flour

1 tablespoon ground cinnamon

¼ teaspoon ground ginger

Banana flakes, for garnish

Makes sixteen 2 × 2-inch bars

A Final Note

Most of us don't think of it, but dietary choices are as important to the brain as they are for any other organ in the body. With every morsel you take in, you're feeding your brain cells either positively or negatively. Plant-based options not only provide essential nutrients to power your cognitive function but also lower your risk of obesity, a health factor linked to declining mental capacity. Living cuisine's low-calorie, low-fat recipes promote lean, healthy eating for optimal weight, which boosts brain health. And when it comes to your immune system, Chapter 6 suggests how eating raw can make you "Armed for Good Health."

ARMED FOR GOOD HEALTH

Your immune system is the mechanism your body employs to prevent and combat disease. It needs to be in tip-top condition to effectively handle the daily assaults, both internal and external, on well-being. Everything you encounter—from the air you breathe to the stressors you experience to the choices you make in life—either compromises or supports good health. (The immune system is fundamental to that preventive medicine we discussed in Chapter 4.)

To ensure that each organ and system of your body remains fit and strong, your immune system relies on a complicated network of cells, tissues, and organs to tailor fighting strategies that protect against infection, chronic disease, and even cancer. Whether it's destroying microbes or curbing ones that can't be eliminated completely, the immune system performs seamlessly. That is, as long as it's healthy, too!

Food That Heals the Healer

Whether you think of it or not, food can have a dramatic impact on defending and healing your body. But you have to make wise choices for it to be a valuable ally in your immune system arsenal. The plant-based foods of living cuisine support the body's natural immune response in a variety of ways.

By offering a great spectrum of antioxidant-rich vitamins, minerals, and enzymes along with amino acids (the building blocks of protein), living foods promote an alkaline environment that supports the immune system in doing its complex health-saving work. (Contrast that to the acidic diet and lifestyle choices that promote disease!)

Among their duties, the antioxidants in living foods help protect and repair cells damaged by free radicals, byproducts of many of the toxins in our modern world. Free radicals interfere with the immune system, contributing to a number of chronic diseases, such as hardening of the arteries, arthritis, lupus, and even cancer. A plant-based diet offers an abundance of benefits that create myriad opportunities for health in the body, oftentimes reversing the damage of free radicals and stopping the overproduction of white blood cells.

Colorful Sources for Soluble Vitamins

What are the best options in a raw-foods diet for supporting your immune and lymphatic systems in their cleansing roles? Many of the fruits, vegetables, and other options you'll adopt with this eating style will help your body fight off infection and disease because they contain important nutrients, especially the antioxidant vitamins C, E, and A (beta-carotene).

These antioxidants represent two families of vitamins—*water-soluble* and *fat-soluble*—that you need to support many body functions. Water-soluble vitamins are absorbed and metabolized quickly, rather than being stored in the cells, so they must be replenished every day. Fat-soluble vitamins dissolve in fat, which means the leftovers are stored in your body. You don't need to replace them every day.

No matter how your body processes them, these nutrients are abundant in colorful fruits and vegetables, so you can't go wrong if you target a mix of raw foods in red, purple, green, orange, or yellow. Your diet and immune system will be better for it!

Vitamin C

A water-soluble vitamin, vitamin C is abundant in:

- Berries
- Cantaloupe
- Kale
- Red, green, and yellow bell peppers
- Strawberries

Vitamin E

A fat-soluble vitamin, vitamin E is found in:

- Chard
- Mustard and turnip greens
- Nuts
- Pumpkin
- Sunflower seeds

Beta-carotene

An essential nutrient that converts into fat-soluble vitamin A, beta-carotene comes from the pigment giving many fruits and vegetables their bright red or orange color. Although carrots are a terrific source, given their deep orange hue, so are:

- Apricots
- Nectarines
- Squash
- Sweet potatoes
- Tangerines

Advice from the Chef

To build a positive immune response in the body:

- Incorporate root vegetables. Beets, yams, carrots, and other such vegetables are rich in minerals that support your body's immune system.

- Try gluten-free grains. Because immune suppression often starts with food allergies, gluten-containing items can diminish your body's healthy response.

- Go light on sweeteners and steer clear of processed sugar. Use stevia in moderation instead.

- Try shiitake mushrooms in soups, salads, and sandwiches. They're the best source of immune support from the mushroom family.

- Enjoy probiotics or fermented foods (page 184) for their body-cleansing powers. They not only are credited with bringing your digestive system into balance but also may bolster your immune function, especially during cold-and-flu season.

Affirmations
for Immune Health

Because your immune system supports every part of your body, you want to support it with every resource possible. Although a living-cuisine lifestyle promotes dietary choices to defend your organs and cells, it also encourages the positive, reinforcing power of thoughts and words. To keep your immune system in the forefront, try these affirmations:

- "I lovingly release all negativity from my body. My body reflects my positive nature."

- "My immune system supports my body. I am strong, healthy, and resilient."

2 apricots (with skin)

1 cup fresh figs (or use
½ cup dried and
reconstitute or soak in
warm water until soft)

1 cup strawberries

¼ cup water

2 tablespoons almond
butter (optional)

1 tablespoon maca root
(optional)

1 teaspoon cinnamon

1 teaspoon dried vanilla
bean (optional)

**Makes
two 12-ounce
servings**

ANTIOXIDANT TONIC

A quick pick-me-up in the morning or as a midafternoon
break, this drink offers a blend of key nutrients—antioxidants, proteins, and essential fatty acids—for supporting
your immune system.

1. Using a blender, combine all the ingredients.

2. Pour into a glass and enjoy.

Note: It's best to enjoy this beverage immediately or within an
hour or two for optimal results. The mixture can also be frozen
and processed later through a Green Star juicer (with blank blade
attachment) for an incredible soft-serve antioxidant-rich yogurt.

GOOD HEALTH GREEN JUICE

As a snack anytime, Good Health Green Juice lends a new twist to an old adage: "A green juice a day keeps the doctor away." At right are three simple variations.

....

1. For each of the juice blends, pass the ingredients through a basic juicer.

2. For maximum benefit, pour into a glass and enjoy immediately.

Note: This juice can be stored for up to 3 days if refrigerated in a single-serving (pint-size) Mason or other canning jar. Fill the jar to the top to minimize oxygen exposure and seal with a lid. The single serving size is important because you don't want to open the jar more than once.

For an apple-celery blend:
1 Red Delicious apple

1 stalk celery

½ hothouse cucumber

1 cup spinach

2 leaves kale

For a spinach-pear blend:
2 cups spinach

1 pear

1 lemon

1-inch piece fresh ginger

For a celery-kale blend:
2 stalks celery

1 leaf kale

1 green apple

1 lime

Makes
1 serving
each

For the dressing:

½ Hass avocado

2 tablespoons lemon juice

2 teaspoons dulse flakes

1 teaspoon chili powder

½ jalapeño pepper (optional)

For the "bowl":

4 cups finely chopped black Tuscan kale, stems removed

2 cups Quinoa Tabbouleh (page 83)

2 cups diced cucumber

½ Hass avocado

1 cup shaved carrot curls*

Makes 1 serving

IMMUNITY BOWL

A blend of kale, quinoa, and other veggies gives this entrée its nutrient punch. With each delicious bite, you're not only creating balance for your endocrine system but also assisting your lymphatic system in removing harmful toxins. Try it for lunch or dinner.

1. To make the dressing, in a blender combine the avocado, lemon juice, dulse flakes, chili powder, and jalapeño. Refrigerate until ready to use.

2. To make the "bowl," in a medium-size mixing bowl, combine the kale, tabbouleh, cucumber, and avocado.

3. Toss with 2 to 4 tablespoons of the dressing, to taste.

4. Plate the salad and top with the carrot curls.

*Carrot curls are easily achieved by running a vegetable peeler the length of a carrot to shave thin pieces.

Note: This dressing can be stored in the refrigerator for up to 3 days for a salad repeat.

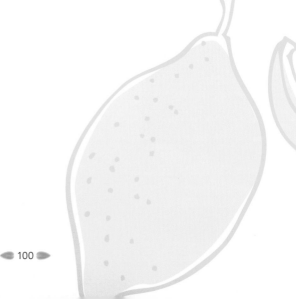

STUFFED SUN-DRIED TOMATOES

Easy to reconstitute, sun-dried tomatoes form the savory basis for this simple snack. The addition of raw garlic, lemon juice, and herbs provides an immune system booster to an appetizer you can enjoy by yourself or share with guests.

....

1. Soak the sun-dried tomato halves in warm water until soft. (Although they'll be dehydrated in a later step, they're hydrated first to fill.)

2. Drain, reserving ⅓ cup of the soaking water.

3. To make the filling, in the food processor, combine the tahini paste, lemon juice, reserved soaking water, scallion, cilantro, garlic, and sea salt. Pulse until combined into a paste.

4. Fill each sun-dried tomato with roughly 2 teaspoons of filling.

5. Line a dehydrator tray with a nonstick surface and dehydrate at 118°F for 2 hours.

6. Remove and garnish with additional cilantro. Enjoy!

Note: You can also use fresh tomatoes for an alternative preparation of this recipe. The tomatoes can be stored in the refrigerator for up to 3 days.

12 sun-dried tomato halves

For the filling:
1 cup raw tahini paste

½ cup lemon juice

⅓ cup soaking water from tomatoes

⅓ cup chopped scallion

⅓ cup chopped cilantro, plus more for garnish

1½ cloves garlic, minced

1 tablespoon sea salt

Makes 12

For the chips:

10 cups chopped curly
kale

4 cups chopped collard
greens

For the marinara:

2 cups chopped
heirloom tomatoes

4 sun-dried tomatoes,
halved

1 clove garlic

1 tablespoon raw agave
nectar or raw honey

2 tablespoons Italian
Blend (page 23)

1 teaspoon sea salt or
1 tablespoon
nutritional yeast

Makes
4 cups

GARLICKY KALE CRISPS

Kale chips are growing in popularity as people learn the
benefits of this ultimate green food. Simple to prepare,
these garlicky crisps can be finished in your dehydrator
or lightly baked in your oven, depending on your preference.

1. To make the chips, in a large bowl, combine the curly
kale and collard greens and toss together.

2. To make the marinara, in a blender combine the heirloom and sun-dried tomatoes, garlic, agave nectar, Italian Blend seasoning, and sea salt and blend until well
combined.

3. Pour the marinara over the greens and toss well. (If
using nutritional yeast, sprinkle over the top at this
point.)

4. Line 2 dehydrator trays with nonstick drying sheets
and disperse the greens evenly.

5. Dehydrate at 118°F for 6 hours, or until crunchy.

Note: An alternative method is to line a cookie sheet with the
crisps and bake at 250°F for 25 minutes, or until crispy. Although
slow baking isn't considered a "raw" preparation technique per
se, it will still yield a plant food snack that's great for transitional
diets, especially when combined with a raw sauce.

BASIC PESTO

This recipe incorporates traditional ingredients for a tasty filling or a cracker and vegetable dip.

....

Mix the olive oil, basil, garlic, and sea salt in a blender until well combined. Add the nuts and blend again. Enjoy.

*Pumpkin seeds can be substituted for the nuts if a diner is nut intolerant.

Note: The pesto can be stored in an airtight container in the refrigerator for up to 2 weeks.

⅓ cup extra-virgin olive oil

½ cup basil

4 to 6 cloves garlic

1 teaspoon sea salt

1 cup pine nuts or pistachios*

Makes 8 ounces

3 cups chopped
   cauliflower

2 cups hot water*

⅓ cup chopped sweet
   yellow onion

¼ cup tahini

1 medium zucchini

1 tablespoon miso paste

1 teaspoon sea salt

¼ cup extra-virgin
   olive oil

Nutritional yeast, to taste

Makes
2 entrée or
4 side-dish
servings

CAULIFLOWER SOUP

A rich and creamy blend, this soup works great for both liquid fasts and cold-weather meals. Packed with vitamins C and K, this dish gets a vitamin B_{12} boost by a sprinkling of nutritional yeast on top.

1. In a blender combine the cauliflower, hot water, onion, tahini, zucchini, miso paste, and sea salt.

2. Blend on high until well combined, being careful not to overheat (see Note).

3. With the machine running, add the olive oil slowly through the feed tube to emulsify the mixture and create a rich, creamy blend.

4. Sprinkle with nutritional yeast before pouring into bowls.

*In living-cuisine prep, 100° to 110°F constitutes "hot"; 80° to 100°F constitutes "lukewarm." Temperatures can be measured easily with a standard candy thermometer.

Note: Heating this soup in a blender will likely require a high-powered model. To test for warmth, keep your hands on the glass container until you feel it, about 2 minutes into the process.

LONGEVITY WRAP

This wrap will quickly become a staple in your raw life-style because it's easy to prepare in advance and then pack for a healthy lunch on the go. Once you're comfortable with the basic recipe, be adventurous and customize it with your own favorite veggies.

....

1. To make the sun-dried tomato ketchup, in a food processor fitted with the S-blade, combine the sun-dried tomatoes, Roma tomato, agave nectar, and sea salt. Process until a thick paste has formed. Transfer to a bowl and set aside.

2. To make the filling, in a medium-size mixing bowl, toss together the broccoli, squash, tomato, red chard, and olives.

3. Lay out the wrapper of your choice and spread with a thin layer of ketchup.

4. Divide the filling evenly between each wrap and roll tightly.

5. Cut on the diagonal and serve up fresh.

Note: Each wrap can be wrapped in parchment paper and stored in the refrigerator for up to 1 day.

2 medium-size collard green leaves (de-stemmed) or 2 nori wraps or 2 sprouted grain tortillas

For the sun-dried tomato ketchup:

1 cup sun-dried tomatoes, soaked in water and drained

1 Roma tomato

1 tablespoon raw agave nectar

1 teaspoon sea salt

For the filling:

1 cup diced broccoli

1 cup diced squash

1 cup diced tomato

1 cup chopped red chard

⅓ cup sliced olives or diced avocado

Makes 2 servings

THAI LIME WRAPS

The filling for this recipe is a two-for-one. You can experience the vegetable, herbal, and spice-rich benefits as the center of a sandwich wrap or as a topper for soup. Either way, the immune-enhancing, digestive-supporting ingredients will warm you at lunch or dinner on a cold day.

1. To make the filling, toss the squash, bean sprouts, Thai coconut flesh, carrot, celery, and slivered nori together in a medium-size bowl.

2. Add the basil, coconut aminos, ginger, coconut oil, cayenne pepper, garlic, and lime juice. Mix until the vegetables are coated.

3. Lay out 2 napa cabbage leaves on a cutting board and fill evenly with one-fourth of the mixture. Roll into a wrap.

4. Repeat with the remaining cabbage leaves and filling.

5. Alternatively, to make the soup, in a blender combine the white miso, celery, scallion, water, ginger juice, and coconut aminos and blend until smooth or slightly chunky, as you prefer.

6. Fill 4 bowls with ¾ cup of the soup mixture.

7. Add one-fourth of the filling to each.

*In living-cuisine prep, 100° to 110°F constitutes "hot"; 80° to 100°F constitutes "lukewarm." Temperatures can be measured easily with a standard candy thermometer.

Note: This recipe is best enjoyed fresh, but the vegetable mixture can be stored in the refrigerator for up to 1 day.

8 medium-size napa cabbage leaves

For the filling:
2 cups julienned crookneck squash or zucchini

2 cups bean sprouts

1 cup young Thai coconut flesh

¼ cup shredded carrot

¼ cup finely chopped celery

1 sheet nori, sliced lengthwise into slivers

2 tablespoons chopped basil

2 tablespoons coconut aminos (an amino acid–rich liquid similar to soy sauce)

1 tablespoon grated ginger

1 tablespoon coconut oil

1 teaspoon cayenne pepper

1 clove garlic, minced

Juice of 1 lime

For the soup:
1 tablespoon mellow white miso

2 stalks celery, chopped

1 scallion, chopped

3 cups hot water*

1 ounce ginger juice

1 ounce coconut aminos

Makes 4 wraps or soup servings

For the marinade:

½ cup extra-virgin olive oil

2 tablespoons raw agave nectar (optional)

2 tablespoons lemon juice

1 tablespoon miso paste

½ clove garlic

For the fusion:

8 cups chopped broccoli

1 cup thinly sliced red onion

½ cup pine nuts or chopped almonds

Makes
4 servings

BROCCOLI FUSION

Good for any season of the year, this dish is a "fusion," or joining, of two vegetables—broccoli and onions—touted for their immune-enhancing capabilities. Even when lightly dehydrated, broccoli maintains its enzyme- and nutrient-rich density. When combined with almonds, red onions, and other healthy ingredients, it makes for a powerful system booster in spring, summer, winter, or fall.

1. To make the marinade, in a blender or using an immersion blender, combine the olive oil, agave nectar, lemon juice, miso paste, and garlic until smooth.

2. To make the fusion, in a medium-size bowl, toss the broccoli, red onion, and pine nuts together; add in the marinade and toss until well coated.

3. Line a dehydrator tray with the broccoli and dehydrate at 118°F for 3 hours. Enjoy.

Note: If you don't have a dehydrator, parboil the broccoli before tossing it with the other ingredients in the marinade. In either case, this dish can be stored in the refrigerator for up to 4 days.

EGGPLANT SPEARS

Italian eggplant provides the perfect lengthwise surface for a dish that's also peppered with immune-enhancing herbs such as cumin, turmeric, and basil. Accompanied by a salad, Eggplant Spears are great as the centerpiece of your family dinner or as a vegetable accompaniment on a company buffet.

1. Slice the eggplant lengthwise.

2. To make the dressing, whisk together the olive oil and sea salt.

3. Brush the dressing on the cut side of the eggplant until the oil is absorbed. Set aside.

4. To make the filling, in a food processor fitted with the S-blade, process the red bell pepper, pesto, turmeric, and cumin until a chutney or relish has formed.

5. Spread the chutney over the spears, coating each.

6. Line a dehydrator tray with a nonstick drying sheet and dehydrate at 118°F for 2 to 4 hours. If you do not have a dehydrator, you can let this recipe sit in the refrigerator to allow the eggplant to soften, and enjoy after about 4 hours.

Note: Because Italian eggplants are smaller than standard eggplants, two pieces constitute a serving in this dish. This dish can be stored in the refrigerator for up to 3 days.

Four 4- to 6-inch Italian eggplants

For the dressing:
6 tablespoons extra-virgin olive oil

1 tablespoon sea salt

For the filling:
1 red bell pepper

2 cups Basic Pesto (page 103)

2 tablespoons turmeric

1 teaspoon cumin

Makes
4 servings

For the dressing:

⅓ cup extra-virgin olive oil

2 tablespoons stone-ground mustard

2 tablespoons raw agave nectar or raw honey

1 teaspoon sea salt

Juice of 1 lemon

For the salad:

2 cups chopped kale

1 cup chopped mustard greens

1 cup chopped collard greens

½ cup dried cranberries (unsweetened)

½ cup walnut pieces

Makes
2 entrée or
4 appetizer
servings

DOWN SOUTH GREENS

This sweet-and-savory salad mixture blends the health-enhancing benefits of kale, mustard greens, and collards. For those new to the dark greens experience, I've added mustard to the dressing to neutralize the bitterness people sometimes taste when introducing these new ingredients to their palate.

1. To make the dressing, in a small bowl, whisk together the olive oil, mustard, agave nectar, sea salt, and lemon.

2. To make the salad, in a medium-size mixing bowl, combine the kale, mustard greens, collard greens, cranberries, and walnut pieces.

3. Pour the dressing onto the greens, toss well, and serve.

Note: This recipe can also be made in advance and stored in the refrigerator for up to 2 days. The dark greens will only soften, becoming even more enjoyable.

THREE-BERRY SALAD

This dish celebrates the multiple nutritious benefits of three different fresh organic berries. Combine blueberries, blackberries, and strawberries with other healthy ingredients for a delicious salad that keeps you energized in the afternoon while supporting your body in dealing effortlessly with stress.

1. Wash the berries well. Combine with the jicama in a medium-size mixing bowl and set aside.

2. To make the dressing, in a blender combine the coconut flesh, water, lemon juice, vanilla bean paste, hemp protein powder, and sea salt. Blend until well emulsified.

3. Fold in the poppy seeds.

4. Toss the berries in the dressing and serve.

Note: This salad can be stored in the refrigerator for up to 5 days.

2 cups blueberries

2 cups blackberries

2 cups strawberries

2 cups shredded jicama or green apple

For the dressing:
¼ cup young Thai coconut flesh

2 tablespoons water

2 tablespoons lemon juice

1 teaspoon vanilla bean paste or dried vanilla bean

1 teaspoon hemp protein powder (optional)

1 teaspoon sea salt

1 teaspoon poppy seeds

Makes four 2-cup servings

CINNAMON TORTES

2 cups pecans

1 tablespoon cinnamon

1 teaspoon nutmeg

3 drops liquid stevia

2 cups dried figs,
reconstituted

1 teaspoon sea salt

Orange slices, dried
cranberries, or
raspberries, for garnish

Makes
twelve
2-inch
tortes

This pecan-and-fig dessert gets its flavorful kick from cinnamon, a popular spice in both traditional and raw diets. By stimulating digestion and supporting the body's immune system, however, cinnamon adds more than just distinctive aroma and flavor to a quick dessert. It's health enhancing and alkaline forming!

1. In a food processor fitted with the S-blade, combine the pecans, cinnamon, nutmeg, and stevia.

2. Pulse the mixture until broken down into a meal.

3. Add the figs and salt, and process until a dough-like mixture has formed.

4. Using a scoop, gently scoop out 12 servings and place on a tray or dish.

5. Press the rounds down softly, creating a round torte.

6. Top each torte with the garnish of your choice and chill until ready to serve.

Note: The tortes can be stored in the refrigerator for up to 1 week. If using fresh fruit, garnish just before serving.

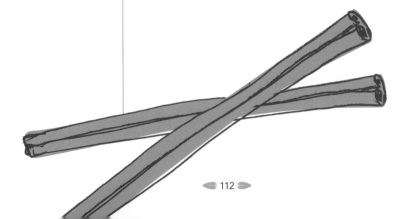

A Final Note

Unless your immune system is healthy, your body doesn't have a fighting chance to ward off infection or disease. It's that simple. You need this intricate network of organs, tissues, and cells to handle assaults from a variety of corners, both inside and outside your body. What's the best way to ensure that your immune system stays strong? Feed it foods that promote an alkaline response so it can fight effectively. By providing antioxidant vitamins and other nutrients through colorful fruits and vegetables, living cuisine supports the immune system in its strategic defense work. Chapter 7, "Healing Your Heart," explains what these colorful components do in the cardiovascular system.

CHAPTER 7

HEALING
YOUR HEART

Few things protect your heart like the food you eat. It's no secret that cardiovascular disease is the number one killer in the U.S. It causes more than half a million (or one in four) deaths a year. Yet research consistently points to food as either facilitating coronary problems or preventing them. Ample scientific evidence, for instance, links a diet high in fat and sugar to the risk factors—elevated blood pressure and "bad" cholesterol—for this disease. That has led at least one cardiovascular disease and prevention expert, Dr. Caldwell B. Esselstyn, Jr., to suggest: "Heart disease is not going to be caused by your genes. It's not going to be caused by your stress. It's not just the luck of the draw. It's a food-borne illness."

A former Cleveland Clinic surgeon, clinician, and researcher, Dr. Esselstyn began his heart-healing work in the mid-1980s after observing lower rates of breast cancer and virtually no heart disease in countries that follow a non-Western diet rich in plant foods. He saw correlations observed by other researchers: Once people native to Africa, rural China, and other cultures adopt the eating patterns of the Western world, they soon see their cholesterol and coronary profiles go bad, too.

Groundbreaking evidence from his subsequent 20-year nutritional study suggests that doctors can prevent, reverse, or stop the progression of heart disease by urging patients to focus on the dietary and lifestyle causes of the disease rather than just treating its symptoms. In doing so, Dr. Esselstyn and his colleagues have witnessed a 90 percent success rate in treating patients once believed to have nonreversible heart disease.

What was behind the amazing turnaround? Study participants experienced positive results by first understanding how they had systematically damaged two critical factors—endothelial cells and nitric oxide—related to their heart health, and then changing their diet and lifestyle to restore them. *Endothelial cells,* a single layer of cells lining your arteries, serve as microscopic insulation, clearing a pathway so your blood can flow freely and your heart can function properly. To do so, they manufacture a magic molecule, called *nitric oxide.* It not only keeps oxygen-rich blood moving smoothly but also prevents the plaque responsible for coronary artery disease and heart attacks.

Over the past several decades, scientists have identified a bevy of high-fat foods, especially animal fats, dairy products, and certain oils, as well as sugar, that damage endothelial cells by interfering with their ability to produce nitric oxide. As the level of nitric oxide becomes reduced, the risk that plaque will mount and obstruct or even rupture the arteries rises.

On the good-news front, scientists have also learned that eliminating animal products and other processed products from your diet can begin the healing. When you stop eating foods injurious to your blood vessels, and replace them with a plant-based menu, your endothelial cells start repairing themselves. Nitric oxide levels are restored. You begin to see a reversal in the risk factors, such as high cholesterol and blood pressure, linked to coronary problems. Most important, heart disease is halted. "When patients see the results and understand that they have control in annihilating this disease," says Dr. Esselstyn, "it can be very empowering."

A Raw-Foods Solution

Which foods, then, are most beneficial for heart health? Because they contain important amino acids, antioxidants, and other phytonutrients, dark leafy green vegetables should top your list. By increasing nitric oxide production and protecting against heart-related illnesses, the green powerhouses arugula, broccoli, mustard or turnip greens, kale, and spinach offer raw-food enthusiasts a spectrum of heart-healing options. In addition, quinoa, buckwheat, cantaloupe, oranges, and all berries are sources of protein, vitamins, and minerals that support heart health.

Even more important, a raw-foods diet eliminates the kind of saturated fat and other oils—corn, safflower, soybean, sunflower, canola, and palm—acknowledged as bad for heart health. But where do plant-based oils—raw olive, hemp, flaxseed, coconut, and avocado—fit in in terms of the heart? The same cautionary rules apply: Avoid them if you already have heart disease. Even though a small amount can be supportive, use them sparingly if you're at risk for heart disease.

The same take-it-easy approach applies to nuts, seeds, and avocado. If you don't have coronary problems and your total cholesterol and low-density lipoproteins, or "LDLs," are below 150 total and 80, respectively, it's fine to incorporate them into your diet. Almonds, pecans, and walnuts, along with hemp, sunflower, chia, and pumpkin seeds, are sources of healthy fat, protein, and fiber. But if you already have heart disease, tread carefully, because these items may increase your cholesterol and they won't reverse your disease. Even though plant-based oils are healthier for the heart than other options, you still have to exercise caution with any fats. So always check with your physician first.

"I believe the best way that a physician can show patients respect is by giving them time. I want to spend the same five hours with patients as a cardiac surgeon. But I want to be with them when they're awake and can fully wrap their arms around what they've been doing to cause this disease. I want them to understand how they've been systematically damaging their endothelial cells and decreasing the levels of nitric oxide so they're empowered to restore both."

— Dr. Esselstyn

Advice from the Chef

To support heart health:

- Add fresh citrus to your daily fare. Grapefruit, oranges, lemons, and limes are naturally fat-free flavorings for many dishes, as well as refreshing snacks.

- Be creative with chopped salads. My favorite is a simple mix of broccoli, green beans, spinach, and diced tomato tossed in a quick blend of lemon juice and mustard.

- Top any salad with simple sweet mustard or other vinaigrettes. By infusing intense flavor into small amounts of raw oil, these dressings are heart-healthy.

- Look to low-fat options such as hummus and other high-protein spreads. Legumes such as lentils can be processed into creamy heart-friendly snacks.

- Make sure dishes such as Garden Gazpacho (page 125) are part of your weekly staples. They're low in oil and high in other nutrients, so you'll experience heart protection.

Affirmations
for the Heart

When it comes to your cardiovascular system, how important is your mental and emotional state to your physical health? According to Michael Miller, M.D., director of the Center for Preventive Cardiology at the University of Maryland Medical Center, it's so critical that, in the future, "it may be possible to incorporate laughter into daily activities, just as is done with other heart-healthy activities such as taking the stairs instead of the elevator. The recommendation for a healthy heart may one day be exercise, eat right, and laugh a few times a day." To get started now, try these mantras:

- *To support overall heart health:* "My heart beats to the rhythm of love."

- *To find peace with any serious heart issue:* "I lovingly allow joy to flow through my mind and body."

For the crust:
2 cups walnut pieces

1 cup buckwheat, sprouted*

½ cup dates

1 tablespoon cinnamon

1 teaspoon sea salt

For the topping:
2 cups fresh fruit of choice

½ cup walnut or almond butter

1 cup coconut flakes

Makes 6 bars

MORNING BLISS BARS

A quick food for launching the day, Morning Bliss Bars support your body by packing various essentials in one place.

1. To make the crust, in a food processor fitted with the S-blade, process the walnut pieces, buckwheat, dates, cinnamon, and sea salt until a dough ball is formed.

2. Press the mixture into a glass loaf pan.

3. To make the topping, in a food processor fitted with the S-blade, process the fruit until a jam-like mixture has formed.

4. Thinly spread the nut butter over the crust, top with the fruit, and sprinkle with the coconut flakes.

5. Cut bars into 6 equal portions and enjoy!

*To sprout raw buckwheat, cover the grains with water and soak for 8 to 12 hours at room temperature. (You'll see tiny tails on the grains.) Rinse and then use.

Note: This dish can be stored in the refrigerator for up to 5 days for an easy breakfast on the go.

KIWI AND GOJI BERRY SALAD

For a colorful potluck dish, try this salad! Just double the recipe or multiply it again, depending on the size of the crowd. Goji berries and kiwi are both high in vitamin C, an antioxidant necessary for many body functions, including supporting and maintaining blood vessels. The hemp seeds supply omega-3 fatty acids.

1. On a cutting board, remove the skin of the kiwi and slice each one in half lengthwise.

2. Place the flat side of each kiwi down on the board and cut them into ½-inch half-moon shapes. Combine with the blueberries, goji berries, and hemp seeds in a medium-size bowl.

3. Squeeze the lemon juice over the salad. Chill in the refrigerator. Drip the stevia and sprinkle the sea salt atop the salad just before serving. Toss lightly and serve chilled.

Note: This salad can be stored in an airtight container in the refrigerator for up to 4 days.

4 medium-size kiwi

1 cup blueberries

1 cup dried goji berries

½ cup hemp seeds

Juice of 1 Meyer
or regular lemon
(optional)

1 drop liquid stevia

Dash of sea salt

Makes
about 3 cups

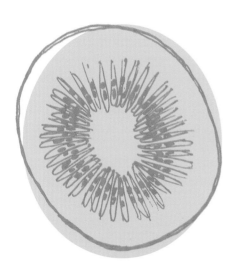

For the salad:

2 cups chopped red chard

2 cups chopped baby romaine lettuce

½ cup thinly sliced red bell pepper

½ cup seasonal vegetables of choice (I love yellow crookneck squash and broccoli, but other options may include mushrooms, cauliflower, eggplant, or celery.)

½ cup steamed quinoa (optional)

For the dressing:

3 tablespoons stone-ground organic mustard

3 tablespoons Meyer lemon juice

3 tablespoons raw apple juice

Pinch of dulse

¼ cup dried banana flakes or pomegranate seeds

MUSTARD SALAD

Featuring a fresh selection of greens in a delightfully crisp mustard dressing, this salad is a go-to choice for the heart-healthy clients on the 118 Degrees restaurants' meal program. In your diet plan, use it as a side for lunch or dinner, or make it the entrée. It can change with the veggies of the season!

1. To make the salad, in a medium-size mixing bowl, combine the red chard, lettuce, red bell pepper, seasonal vegetables, and quinoa; toss together well.

2. To make the dressing, in a small bowl, whisk together the mustard, lemon juice, apple juice, and dulse until well blended. Pour over the salad and toss well.

3. Garnish with the banana flakes and enjoy!

Makes
2 servings

TANGERINE BEET SLAW

Chock-full of nutrients—vitamin C, folate, potassium, and magnesium—that support a healthy heart, this salad is a recipe for averting coronary artery disease. Tangerines and beets come together in a dish that can be used as a side, as an appetizer with crackers, or as the filling of a buckwheat wrap.

....

1. In a medium-size mixing bowl, toss together the beets, scallion, orange juice, and sea salt. Let sit for 15 minutes.

2. Just before serving, toss the avocado and tangerines together lightly in another medium-size mixing bowl.

3. In a circular mold with a removable top piece, layer the beet and avocado-tangerine mixtures to create a stack. Gently invert the mold and remove the top, pressing the contents onto a plate.

4. Garnish the plate with additional scallion.

Note: The slaw can be stored without the avocado in the refrigerator for up to 3 days; add fresh avocado just before serving.

2 cups shredded beets

½ cup chopped scallion, plus more for garnish

¼ cup fresh orange juice (raw unpasteurized fresh tangerine juice works well, too, if it's available!)

1 teaspoon sea salt

¼ cup diced avocado

2 cups tangerine slices

Makes
4 servings

6 tomatillos

½ cup water

¼ cup chopped red onion

3 tablespoons chopped cilantro leaves, plus more for garnish

2 teaspoons sea salt

1 clove garlic

Juice of 2 serrano peppers, extracted using a juicer

Carrot shreds, for garnish

Makes 4 servings

SPICY TOMATILLO SOUP

Oil- and sugar-free but still flavorful, this soup relies on a Mexican edible that grows readily in the American Southwest. The tomatillo—a greenish-purple fruit, sized between a cherry tomato and an apricot—provides the hearty and heart-healthy foundation for this spicy, satisfying lunch or dinner entrée.

1. In a blender combine the tomatillos, water, red onion, cilantro leaves, sea salt, garlic, and serrano pepper juice; blend until well combined.

2. Ladle the soup into bowls and garnish with additional cilantro and the shredded carrot.

Note: This soup can be stored in the refrigerator for up to 4 days.

GARDEN GAZPACHO

A "garden of health," this chilled soup is packed with fresh vegetables and herbs, so it's also replete with a variety of vitamins, minerals, and other phytonutrients. A puree that's both filling and flavorful, Garden Gazpacho can be served during every season. If tomatoes aren't available, just double the red bell pepper.

....

1. In a blender combine the tomato, cucumber, red bell pepper, water, basil, garlic, lemon juice, and sea salt. Blend until well combined.

2. Ladle the soup into bowls and garnish with the asparagus and chard.

Note: This soup can be stored in the refrigerator for up to 4 days.

2 cups chopped tomato

2 cups chopped cucumber

1 cup chopped red bell pepper

½ cup water

½ cup chopped fresh basil

2 cloves garlic

2 tablespoons lemon juice

1 teaspoon sea salt

½ cup shaved asparagus, for garnish

½ cup chopped red chard, for garnish

Makes
4 servings

6 small napa cabbage leaves

For the cauliflower puree:
3 cups lightly steamed cauliflower florets

½ cup hot water*

2 tablespoons chopped parsley

1 teaspoon miso paste

For the topping:
½ cup thinly sliced red onion

2 tablespoons coconut aminos

2 cups diced heirloom tomato

2 cups chopped spinach

Makes
6 servings

CABBAGE CUPS WITH CAULIFLOWER PUREE

Eating a heart-healthy diet doesn't have to be boring! It's easy to add a little flair to your menu with a dish that blends the vegetable staples you know—cauliflower, tomatoes, and red onions—with a few new tastes.

1. To make the cauliflower puree, in a food processor fitted with the S-blade, combine the cauliflower, hot water, parsley, and miso paste. Pulse until pureed.

2. To make the topping, in a medium-size mixing bowl, combine the red onion and coconut aminos. Toss and let stand for a few minutes until the onion begins to soften.

3. Add the diced tomato and spinach, and toss.

4. Place the cabbage leaves on a cutting board. Line each spine with one-sixth of the cauliflower puree. Top with one-sixth of the topping mixture. Serve at room temperature.

*In living-cuisine prep, 100° to 110°F constitutes "hot"; 80° to 100°F constitutes "lukewarm." Temperatures can be measured easily with a standard candy thermometer.

Note: This dish can be stored in the refrigerator for up to 3 days. Store the components separately or assembled.

For the marinade:

½ cup coconut aminos

½ cup coconut water

1 red bell pepper, cored
and seeded

1 clove garlic

1 teaspoon miso paste

1 teaspoon chili powder

Juice of 1 lemon

For the vegetable mixture:

4 cups chopped broccoli

2 cups julienned zucchini

1 cup shredded carrot

1 cup finely chopped
napa cabbage

1 cup de-stemmed,
chopped shiitake
mushrooms

Makes
2 entrée or
4 side-dish
servings

TOSSED MARINATED BROCCOLI BOWL

The beauty of this broccoli dish is that it's not only a culinary plus for heart-healthy-minded individuals but tasty, too. Whether served as an entrée or introduced as a side, this marinated broccoli combo offers a flavor and texture duo that's a sure winner.

1. To make the marinade, combine the coconut aminos, coconut water, red bell pepper, garlic, miso paste, chili powder, and lemon juice in a blender. Blend until combined.

2. To make the vegetable mixture, in a large mixing bowl, combine the broccoli, zucchini, carrot, cabbage, and shiitake mushrooms and toss together well.

3. Pour the marinade over the mixture and toss well.

Variation: Add sesame seeds for extra flavor or cayenne pepper for more spice!

Note: This dish can be stored in the refrigerator for up to 3 days.

ROLLED STREET TACOS

A heart-healthy variation on a common lunch and snack theme, these tacos blend dark leafy greens, a variety of vegetables, and red bell peppers into a filling treat. The ingredients bring together many of the nutrients, such as folate and vitamin B_6, that your blood vessels need to function!

2 cups chopped red bell pepper

2 cups chopped red chard leaves and stems

1 cup peeled and diced tomatillos

½ cup chopped cilantro leaves

¼ cup chopped scallion

1 teaspoon sea salt

1 clove garlic, minced

2 cups diced avocado

2 cups diced mushrooms

4 small collard green leaves

1. In a food processor fitted with the S-blade, combine the red bell pepper, chard, tomatillos, cilantro, scallion, sea salt, and garlic. Pulse the ingredients until a chunky salsa-like texture is achieved.

2. Add the avocado and mushrooms. Lightly pulse until combined.

3. De-stem each collard green leaf.

4. Fill the center of each leaf with one-fourth of the mixture. Roll up each taco and enjoy right away.

Note: These tacos can be stored in the refrigerator for up to 2 days.

Makes
4 servings

2 cups quinoa, sprouted*

2 cups diced butternut squash

½ cup water

2 cloves garlic, chopped

¼ cup chili powder

1 tablespoon sea salt

4 cups thinly sliced sweet onion

Makes
12 crackers

BUTTERNUT SQUASH AND SWEET ONION CRACKERS

A delicious oil-free snack, this tangy option serves as a great base for appetizers or an accompaniment for crudités.

1. In a blender combine the quinoa, butternut squash, and water. Blend.

2. Add the garlic, chili powder, and salt. Blend again.

3. In a medium-size mixing bowl, combine the onion and butternut mixture; toss together well.

4. Prepare 2 dehydrator trays with your choice of non-stick surface.

5. Scoop out twelve 2-tablespoon portions of the mixture and place evenly on the trays; flatten each scoop into ¼-inch-thick rounds, approximately 3 inches in diameter.

6. Dehydrate the crackers at 118°F for 12 hours, gently lifting and flipping the crackers halfway through the process.

7. Remove from the dehydrator and let cool.

*To sprout raw quinoa, cover the quinoa with water and soak for 8 to 12 hours at room temperature. (You'll see tiny tails on the grains.) Rinse and then use.

Note: These crackers can be stored in an airtight container in the pantry indefinitely.

HEART CAKES

Light fats come together with antioxidant-boosting ber-ries to produce a delicious and invigorating snack or treat. I use a 4-inch cutter, but feel free to go smaller or larger.

2 cups coconut flour

½ cup coconut water

2 cups raspberries or strawberries

4 drops liquid stevia

1 teaspoon vanilla bean paste*

1 teaspoon sea salt

Makes 9 to 12 squares

1. In a food processor fitted with the S-blade, pulse the coconut flour and water until well combined.

2. Add 1 cup of the berries along with the stevia, vanilla bean paste, and sea salt. Process until a dough-like mix-ture has formed.

3. Pat the mixture into an 8 × 8-inch glass dish. Slice or mash the remaining 1 cup berries in a small dish to cre-ate a topping for the cakes. Set aside.

4. Taking a small heart-shaped cookie cutter, cut out hearts and arrange them on a silicone-lined dehydrator tray. Dehydrate the cakes at 115°F for 4 hours.** Remove the cakes and top with the fresh berries.

*If you don't have vanilla bean paste, substitute natural vanilla flavoring but not pure vanilla extract. It contains alcohol, which doesn't translate well taste-wise.

**Even without a dehydrator, you can still enjoy this recipe. The crust will just be softer than a dehydrated shell.

Note: This dish can be stored in the refrigerator for up to 1 week.

2 cups chopped fresh fruit (I love pineapple, but you can also use kiwi, mango, passionfruit, peaches, berries of any sort, oranges, and other citrus fruits.)

3 frozen bananas

1 cup walnuts (optional)

2 tablespoons Warrior Food or other plant-based protein supplement (optional)

2 cups Creative Crunchy Granola (page 76) or steel-cut oats

2 cups pomegranate seeds

Makes
4 servings

POMEGRANATE PARFAITS

With antioxidant-filled pomegranate seeds, this parfait is a fun way to fuel your heart. A summer favorite, it's also a fresh take on the standard whipped dessert. Enjoy it with a glass of sparkling tea at your next garden party, and toast your vibrant health! If you're so inspired, try it for breakfast, too!

1. Chill the chopped fruit until ready to use.

2. Using a blender, blend the frozen bananas until a thick ice cream–like chopped texture is achieved.

3. Add the walnuts and protein powder.

4. In a parfait glass, layer 2 tablespoons banana, 2 tablespoons fruit, 2 tablespoons granola, and 2 tablespoons pomegranate seeds.

5. Repeat this process 3 times, filling up the glass.

Note: You can refreeze banana leftovers to use the following day.

For the cacao crème:
1 Hass avocado

½ cup coconut water (or regular water)

½ cup raw cacao powder

½ cup raw agave nectar

Pinch of sea salt

For the cake mixture:
2 cups pecans or walnuts

½ cup raw cacao powder

1 tablespoon cinnamon

1 teaspoon sea salt

⅓ cup raw agave nectar

4 cups mixed berries (strawberries, blueberries, raspberries, or others of your choice), plus ½ cup, sliced, for garnish

Makes 8 servings

CHOCOLATE BERRY TRIFLE

My grandmother always attended dinner parties with a giant trifle in hand. I'm not sure which I remember more—the beautiful crystal bowl, the scrumptious-looking layers, or the incredible berry topping—but when it landed on our table, we were in for a treat. Grandma's classic trifle is the inspiration for this healthy dessert. This one is great for sharing, too!

1. To make the cacao crème, combine the avocado, coconut water, raw cacao powder, raw agave nectar, and sea salt in a blender and blend well. Place in the refrigerator while preparing the rest of the dish.

2. To make the cake mixture, in a food processor fitted with the S-blade, chop the nuts until a fine meal has formed.

3. Add the cacao powder, cinnamon, and sea salt, and blend again.

4. Add the agave nectar and process until a ball has formed.

5. To assemble in a trifle bowl, layer one-third of the cake mixture, followed by 1⅓ cups of the mixed berries, and then one-third of the crème. Repeat 2 more times until all the ingredients are used.

6. Garnish with the fresh sliced berries.

A Final Note

For decades, research has linked what you eat with the major risk factors for cardiovascular disease. In fact, one scientist's groundbreaking nutritional study demonstrates that by focusing patients on changing their dietary and lifestyle choices, rather than just treating symptoms, physicians *can* make significant progress in preventing, reversing, and even stopping heart disease. Because plant-based foods are rich in heart-healthy nutrients and low in heart-unhealthy fats, they're an excellent first step in this process. But what can they do for other conditions? As Chapter 8 suggests, there are undeniable benefits in "Eating 'Raw' for Diabetes."

EATING "RAW" FOR DIABETES

If you have diabetes, you already know that food and lifestyle choices can affect your blood sugar. But what does a plant-based diet bring to the table? Besides eliminating high fats and acidic foods, it offers many of the nutrients you need to forge a healthy body while controlling type 1 or type 2 forms of this chronic and potentially life-threatening disease.

A balanced diet of "raw" vegetables, fruits, whole grains (quinoa and buckwheat, for starters), and legumes (dried beans, peas, and lentils) yields a multitude of vitamins, minerals, protein, complex carbohydrates, and fiber. Not only do these choices offer tremendous general healing and anti-inflammatory capabilities, but they're also low-calorie

and low-glycemic. That means they keep obesity, a critical diabetes cofactor, at bay while ensuring that blood glucose reaches and stays as close to normal as possible.

Because of such results, one prominent holistic physician, Gabriel Cousens, M.D., believes that a plant-based diet is a natural way to improve diabetes, particularly type 2, and actually *heal* it. *Healing* for some 180 diabetics who've participated in his 21-day medically supervised nutritional program means that they're off insulin or other oral medications with an acceptable fasting blood sugar level of less than 100. That group includes non-insulin-dependent and insulin-dependent type 2 diabetics (those who fail to process insulin normally) as well as individuals with prediabetes. It has also generated positive effects for some type 1 diabetics, people who don't produce the blood-regulating hormone, let alone process it.

These numbers may seem very small compared to the 26 million Americans who have either type 1 or type 2 diabetes. But Dr. Cousens has witnessed enough improvement at his Patagonia, Arizona, Tree of Life Rejuvenation Center to see his protocol as a treatment option for people with diabetes, prediabetes, or even a predisposition to blood sugar imbalances. The key to its success lies in strict adherence to an individualized regimen, which favors low-glycemic greens and other veggies plus nuts and seeds. The diet features 25 to 45 percent healthy plant-based fats, 25 to 35 percent plant-based complex carbohydrates, and 25 to 35 percent plant-based proteins. Participants are supervised during a weeklong detoxification and then monitored daily during two weeks of dietary, nutritional, and lifestyle classes. Nursing support continues for a year after the 21-day stay.

Even if you're not participating in such a structured program, you can still experience the blood-sugar-regulating benefits of living cuisine. Because diet (and the way it affects genes) plays a major role in this disease, modifying your eating pattern is an important part of care. Raw foods, by their very nature, promote nutrition, healthy weight, and alkalinity. They can be a positive force in keeping your blood sugar in check.

Advice from the Chef

To control blood glucose:

- Green is good, so rotate green juice, green smoothies, and green salads throughout the week to help regulate your metabolism and blood sugar. Keep it interesting by pairing options, such as avocado with kale, ginger with green juice, and blueberries in other smoothies.

- Concentrate on sea vegetables as green sources. Although they may represent a new taste and texture, they're easy to add to many dishes. For starters, sprinkle dulse flakes (red seaweed) on your salads for extra minerals and B vitamins.

- Substitute an avocado spread for creamy dressings and butters to eliminate dairy from your diet. You'll still enjoy rich flavor and texture, minus the negatives.

- Incorporate superfoods and nut-milk-based blends, such as almond or coconut milk, into your snack menu. Besides convenience, they offer sugar-stabilizing abilities and easily absorbed nutrients, such as essential fats.

- Learn to love quinoa. Technically a seed, this whole-grain plant protein doubles as a complex carbohydrate. Because it's also naturally gluten-free, it won't spike your insulin levels but can be a great grain for keeping your glucose in line.

Affirmations
for Diabetes Healing

It's been said that loving yourself and developing strong emotional ties play an important role in health and healing. I agree. Detoxifying yourself of negative influences while supporting the positives in life can help you achieve inner peace and overall wellness. Dr. Cousens is famous for saying, "The key factor for success is loving yourself enough to want to heal yourself." Healing indeed begins within by both what you eat and how you feel.

- *To heal from diabetes:* "Miracles happen every day. I go within to dissolve the pattern that created this, and I now accept a divine healing. And so it is."

- *To move forward with your disease:* "I am enthusiastic about life and filled with energy."

BRAZIL NUT MILK SHAKE

Brazil nuts are high in selenium, a mineral that helps regulate metabolism and blood sugar. They also give this shake a unique flavor profile, pairing nicely with the spices. If you don't have Brazil nuts, any nut or seed milk will yield great results with this recipe.

....

1. To make the nut milk, in a blender combine the water and Brazil nuts. Blend until well combined.

2. Strain through a strainer or cheesecloth and separate the remaining pulp from the milk. (The pulp may be stored to dehydrate into flour.)

3. To make the shake, combine all the ingredients in a blender. Blend well until a thick shake is achieved.

4. You may add ½ cup of ice to create a cold, frothy shake. The shake may also be frozen into ice cubes to integrate into any morning smoothie.

*Brazil nuts should be soaked in water overnight or about 8 hours and then rinsed. Use within 48 hours.

Note: Enjoy the shake within an hour of preparation for maximum benefit. You may also elect to add ½ cup of spinach or 1 tablespoon of supergreen powder to further aid in metabolism support.

For the nut milk:
2 cups water

½ cup soaked Brazil nuts*

For the shake:
1 cup Brazil nut milk

1 persimmon or pear or ½ cup chopped pumpkin

1 tablespoon maca root (optional)

1 tablespoon cinnamon

1 teaspoon nutmeg

Makes two 8-ounce servings

⅓ cup lemon or lime juice

3 tablespoons extra-virgin olive oil

1 tablespoon dark chili powder

1 teaspoon sea salt

2 cups sliced nopales

1 cup shredded carrot

1 cup julienned squash

⅓ cup thinly sliced red onion

⅓ cup chopped red bell pepper (optional)

3 tablespoons chopped cilantro

3 tablespoons chopped scallion

2 cups organic mixed greens

2 tablespoons hemp or pumpkin seeds (optional, for protein)

½ cup Avocado Citrus Dressing (recipe on page 143)

Makes
2 servings

NOPALITOS SALAD

The nopales cactus leaf is excellent for maintaining healthy blood sugar levels. This fresh salad can be prepared in advance for use throughout the week and may be added as a topping or taco filling as well.

1. In a small mixing bowl, whisk together the lemon juice, olive oil, chili powder, and sea salt. Mix in the nopales. Let stand while preparing the rest of the salad. Ideally, this mixture becomes more enjoyable while the citrus juice works to soften the nopales.

2. In a medium-size mixing bowl, combine the carrot, squash, red onion, red bell pepper, cilantro, and scallion.

3. Add the nopales mixture to the vegetable mixture and toss well to combine.

4. Set the salad mixture atop the mixed greens and garnish with the hemp seeds. Drizzle with the Avocado Citrus Dressing.

Note: The salad mixture can be stored separately in the refrigerator for up to 4 days. Just before serving, place atop the greens and drizzle with the dressing.

AVOCADO CITRUS DRESSING

A refreshing topping for any dish, this vinaigrette combines the nutrient punch of avocado and orange juice.

....

Whisk together all the ingredients in a bowl or blend in a blender.

½ Hass avocado, peeled and pitted

½ cup coconut water

¼ cup orange juice

1 tablespoon raw honey

Makes
½ cup

4- to 5-inch piece lotus root

1 yellow crookneck squash or zucchini, chopped

1 scallion, chopped, plus ⅓ cup chopped scallion, for garnish

2 cups hot water*

1 tablespoon red or white miso

1 tablespoon tahini

½ cup chopped fresh vegetable of choice, such as red bell pepper, tomato, avocado, or asparagus

⅓ cup chopped sea vegetable (optional)

Makes 2 servings

LOVING LOTUS SOUP

A Chinese medicinal staple for supporting the endocrine system and balancing the digestive tract, lotus root has many uses in a raw-foods diet. It can be juiced, steeped for tea, or sliced paper-thin as an ingredient for this and other recipes. Loving Lotus Soup is a twist on traditional miso soup, but with a little thicker consistency and added nutritional benefits.

1. Cut off 3 inches from the lotus root and pass through a basic juicer. Slice the remaining 1 or 2 inches of lotus root into paper-thin slices to float in the soup. (The heat from your soup will quickly soften the lotus root.)

2. In a blender combine the lotus root juice, squash, the 1 chopped scallion, hot water, miso, and tahini. Process until blended to a thick consistency.

3. Pour the soup into 2 bowls and top with the remaining ⅓ cup chopped scallion, chopped fresh vegetable, sea vegetable, and sliced lotus root.

*In living-cuisine prep, 100° to 110°F constitutes "hot"; 80° to 100°F constitutes "lukewarm." Temperatures can be measured easily with a standard candy thermometer.

Note: This soup can be stored in the refrigerator for up to 1 day.

ROLLED SQUASH SNACKS

Because these wraps can be made in 5 minutes or less, using a whisk and a mandoline, they're perfect as a quick, healthy snack. Prepare them in advance or at the last minute for a tasty afternoon interlude.

1. To make the sauce, whisk together the tahini, lemon juice, Italian Blend seasoning, and sea salt in a bowl until well combined.

2. To make the filling, in a medium-size bowl combine the spinach, tomato, carrot, quinoa, and olives. Mix well. Add the sauce and toss to combine.

3. On a cutting board, slice the zucchini lengthwise using a mandoline set at ¼ inch thick. This should create 12 slices of squash.

4. To create the wrap, place 3 squash slices next to each other lengthwise so the edges overlap slightly.

5. Spread ⅔ cup of the filling along the center of the three pieces.

6. Wrap or roll the squash pieces around the mixture tightly so you can pick up the snack with your fingers.

7. Repeat for the remaining 3 wraps.

*To steam raw quinoa, place the quinoa in a steamer basket over a pot of water on the stove and steam for 7 minutes if presoaked and 15 minutes if not. To sprout, cover the quinoa with water and soak for 8 to 12 hours at room temperature. (You'll see tiny tails on the grains.) Rinse and then use.

1 large zucchini

For the sauce:
⅓ cup tahini

⅓ cup lemon juice

1 tablespoon Italian Blend (page 23)

1 teaspoon sea salt

For the filling:
1 cup chopped spinach or red chard

1 cup diced tomato

½ cup shredded carrot or beet

½ cup quinoa, steamed or sprouted*

⅓ cup diced olives or fresh avocado

Makes
4 wraps

16 cups curly kale

1 Roma tomato

3 cups water

2 cups pumpkin seeds, soaked

½ cup lemon juice

2 tablespoons 118 Spices* or seasoning blend of your choice (page 23)

2 tablespoons nutritional yeast (optional)

1 tablespoon sea salt

Makes 8 servings

PUMPKIN SEED KALE CRISPS

Although these crisps are best prepared in the dehydrator, you can bake them in the oven at a low temperature. You'll sacrifice some of the nutritional benefits, but you'll have a snack alternative to basic crackers and chips.

1. Wash and chop the kale into roughly 4 × 4-inch pieces.

2. In a blender add the tomato, water, pumpkin seeds, lemon juice, seasoning, nutritional yeast, and sea salt. Blend until well combined.

3. Place the kale in a large bowl. Pour the mixture on top and toss together until the kale is well coated.

4. Line 3 dehydrator trays with nonstick drying sheets and spread out the kale evenly.

5. Dehydrate at 118°F for 15 hours. (If preparing in an oven, preheat to 250°F and bake for 1 hour.)

*118 Spices is a restaurant favorite that can be purchased through www.118degrees.com.

Note: The crisps can be stored in an airtight container in the pantry indefinitely.

A Final Note

As with heart disease, controlling diabetes relies heavily on lifestyle choices. You can't keep your blood sugar levels under control if you don't select foods and activities that support a healthy outcome. Research repeatedly links good choices with good results. But what can a raw-foods diet actually do for *you*? Dr. Cousens believes plant-based foods alone can heal diabetes in some sufferers, as he has witnessed firsthand. You may not undergo the medically supervised nutritional program that's produced such results, but you can still experience the plusses of eating nutrient-plentiful, low-calorie, and low-glycemic plant-based foods. What else can they do? As Chapter 9 explains, eating raw can also help in "Strengthening Your Frame."

STRENGTHENING YOUR FRAME

You may not think about it, but the musculoskeletal system giving you stature, strength, and mobility is a living force. As such, it must be fed daily. But can you get the quality vitamins, minerals, amino acids/proteins, and carbohydrates needed to bolster your physical structure from plant-based foods? Absolutely! Many incredible vegan athletes have discovered that a raw-foods diet of dark leafy greens, nuts, lentils, seeds, and other high-protein items supplies the necessary nutrients to keep bones, muscles, and joints, together with tendons, ligaments, and cartilage, strong and healthy!

Built and Nourished to Last

From head to toe, your skeleton supports and protects every part of your body, even giving some parts, like your skull, their distinctive shape. Although each bone has a specific function, they're all composed of living tissue that's continually renewed, repaired, and reshaped by specialized cells. The same goes for your body's muscles and connective tissues (ligaments, tendons, and cartilage). Besides holding the skeleton together, they facilitate every conscious or voluntary move you make.

As strong as your musculoskeletal system is, however, parts of it can weaken, break, or become damaged. Overuse, injury, aging, and disease can cause many issues. But some skeletal damage can be directly related to food. Calcium and vitamin insufficiencies, for instance, contribute to osteoporosis, a thinning of the bones that leads to brittleness and easy breaks. Similarly, the painful and stiff joints of arthritis result from inflammation, which is brought on or made worse by a diet high in acidic foods, among other factors.

Plant-based foods can yield positive results for these and other musculoskeletal problems. In addition to helping you manage your weight, which in excess can put undue stress on your frame, plant-based foods contain the vital nutrients your physical structure needs to remain strong, operate effectively, and protect against injury or disease. Nutrients help your bones, muscles, and connective tissue undergo the restoration necessary to function superbly for years.

Foods That Feed Your Structure

Raw foods help your musculoskeletal system by providing functional building blocks with every meal. In fact, what's truly unique about a plant-based eating style is that every dish serves the body, including your physical structure. By balancing your menu each day with anti-inflammatory choices, you're minimizing the impact of acid buildup. You're also making sure that your bones, muscles, and connective tissue get the nutrients—vitamins, minerals, proteins/amino acids, and carbohydrates—they need. Coupling high-enzyme living fruits and vegetables with the amino acids in hemp and chia seeds, for instance, helps stimulate cellular regeneration, which speeds healing. Although plant-based foods produce a mixture of nutrients, you need certain ones more than others to support your physical structure.

— **Vitamins.** Vitamin C promotes healthy bones by boosting the synthesis of collagen, the tissue that binds cells together, and stimulating alkaline phosphatase, an enzyme involved in the creation of bone-building cells. Plant-based sources include red berries, kiwi, tomatoes, spinach, and bell peppers along with oranges, grapefruit, and guava juices. Similarly, vitamin K, which is found in leafy green vegetables, plays a role in ensuring that the proteins involved in bone health are functioning correctly. And by helping the body absorb calcium, vitamin D helps strengthen the skeleton. Although it can be found in a few living-cuisine foods such as mustard greens and white mushrooms, sunlight is the best natural source. Vitamin D is unique in that your body manufactures it when rays hit your skin. But here's the catch: To trigger production, you'd need to bask sunscreen-free in direct sunlight for 10 to 15 minutes each day during prime hours. That may not be expedient or wise, depending on where you live and the fact that you'd be exposing yourself to a potentially higher risk of skin cancer. So to achieve the vitamin D benefits, you'll likely need to incorporate supplements into your daily diet.

— **Minerals.** Calcium helps your bones grow strong when you're young, and it helps prevent bone loss or breaks from osteoporosis later in life. Trace amounts of other minerals, such as iron, magnesium, phosphorus, potassium, and zinc, are also necessary for your bones and muscles to function and maintain strength. Even though calcium is abundant in dairy products, it's also plentiful in plant-based sources: dark leafy greens and veggies, broccoli, and Brussels sprouts, along with chickpeas, sesame seeds, almond or soy milk, soybeans, tofu, and even freshly squeezed orange juice. These foods have the added value of not being tainted by the steroids, antibiotics, and other growth hormones typically found in dairy products, which can actually hurt your physical structure.

— **Amino acids.** The building blocks of protein, these powerhouse essentials help your musculoskeletal structure achieve strength, endurance, and muscular mass. Because your body doesn't make 9 of the 20 or so known amino acids required for manufacturing protein, you need to import them. (They're referred to as *essential* because adding them *is* essential!)

A plant-based diet can yield your daily requirements of these nine essential amino acids. Nearly all living vegetables, beans, grains, nuts, and seeds contain some, if not significant amounts of, essential amino acids. Some foods—such as chia, hemp, and pumpkin seeds, along with quinoa—are considered complete, high-protein sources because they offer substantial amounts of amino acids. Other plant foods contribute only part of what you need daily. But eating a balanced plant-based selection that meets your energy needs can yield enough amino acids in total to build protein for healthy muscles, connective tissue, and bones.

— **Carbohydrates.** Although carbohydrates are known for helping energize the body and fuel the brain, they also play a role in promoting both bone and muscle strength. Research has shown that complex carbohydrates help improve bone mass density and may even aid in the absorption of calcium. They also help muscles recover after exercise by converting glycogen to usable energy, contributing to weight loss. Complex carbohydrates are abundant in many of the same raw fruits, vegetables, legumes, and whole grains that supply other musculoskeletal-strengthening nutrients.

Advice from the Chef

To build strong bones:

- Enjoy high-protein foods such as hemp and chia seeds daily.

- Make sure with each meal of the day that you're achieving the nutritional basics your bones and muscles need: essential fats, proteins, vitamins, and minerals. To accomplish this task, make a salad or smoothie from avocado, hemp seeds, almonds, chopped spinach or kale, and fresh berries.

- Integrate coconut butter by spreading the paste on fresh fruit or mixing it with raw cacao for a simple, enticing dessert. It's a great staple for a healthy body.

- Include sea vegetables and tahini in your salads. They're a great source of the calcium and B vitamins needed by both muscles and bones.

- Eat like a gorilla. Dark leafy greens, such as kale, collards, and chard, make great "wraps." When paired with seed cheese, these vibrant veggies can produce a balanced meal.

Affirmations
for a Strong Body

Keeping your bones and muscles fortified takes a daily commitment to musculoskeletal-friendly foods. You need a balance of nutrients to ensure that your frame develops well and remains strong. But staying focused on good bone and muscular health sometimes gets lost in life's daily shuffle. Below are examples to remind yourself.

- "My physical body is growing stronger every day."

- "My body effortlessly uses all the nutrients I supply to create a strong physical structure."

WARRIOR MYLK

By combining the nutrient clout of hemp, spirulina, and a protein superpowder, this drink is a quick and easy way to strengthen and support your skeletal and muscular systems. As a daily pick-me-up, Warrior Mylk makes me feel superenergetic!

1. Using a blender, combine all the ingredients. Blend well into a rich, thick milk.

2. Pour into a glass and enjoy, or refrigerate for a milk shake experience.

Note: This drink can be stored in the refrigerator for up to 1 week.

8 ounces hemp milk or coconut milk

2 tablespoons coconut butter or ½ cup young Thai coconut flesh

2 tablespoons protein superpowder or soaked chia seeds

1 tablespoon spirulina

¼ teaspoon vanilla flavoring or vanilla paste

1 drop liquid stevia or 1 date

Probiotics of choice (Follow package instructions for amount.)

Makes one 8-ounce serving

6 ounces fresh berries or
frozen wild blueberries

1 cup raw apple juice or
coconut water

½ cup young Thai
coconut flesh or
2 tablespoons coconut
butter

1 medium-size pear,
seeded and roughly
chopped

2 tablespoons chia seeds

1 tablespoon maca root

2 tablespoons raw cacao
powder (optional, for
energy)

1 teaspoon vanilla paste
(optional)

Makes two
8-ounce
servings

BERRY REGENERATOR SMOOTHIE

This smoothie balances plant-based proteins, amino acids, and essential minerals in a fortifying liquid meal to be enjoyed alone or alongside other foods. Incorporated for endurance, the chia seeds add a sweetness akin to poppy seeds to this rich, creamy smoothie.

In a blender combine all the ingredients. Blend until smooth and enjoy within 1 hour.

Note: Because the chia seeds also serve as a thickener, this recipe can be stored in the refrigerator for up to 2 days and enjoyed as a yogurt in a parfait.

FRUIT MAGIC

This basic fruit plate brings together the nutritional strengths of melon, figs, hemp seeds, avocado, and berries in a dish that supports your whole body. Combine them for a refreshing option for lunch. Later in the day, follow with a meal that is high in essential fatty acids to balance blood sugar.

....

1. Remove the rinds of the melon and arrange lengthwise across a plate.

2. Top with the fresh berries, then the diced avocado.

3. In a small mixing bowl, toss together the figs and hemp seeds and sprinkle on the fruit.

Four ½-inch-thick slices seasonal melons

For the topping:
1 cup fresh berries of choice

½ Hass avocado, diced

¼ cup chopped figs

3 tablespoons hemp seeds

Makes
1 serving

For the sauce:
1 medium-size Hass
   avocado

1 cup young Thai
   coconut flesh or
   2 tablespoons coconut
   butter

⅓ cup water

2 tablespoons lemon
   juice

2 tablespoons raw honey
   or 2 drops liquid stevia

1 teaspoon sea salt

For the salad:
4 Granny Smith apples

½ cup goji berries,
   soaked in water to
   cover

¼ cup hemp seeds
   (optional, for additional
   protein)

Makes 4
appetizer
servings

GREEN APPLE SALAD

Unlike traditional Waldorf or apple salads, which use dairy-rich sauces as a binder, this living-cuisine option relies on avocado and coconut to create a thick, creamy sauce. A beautiful accompaniment to soups and a great topping for a basic green salad, it can also be used as a filling in wraps or as a snack on crackers. It's that versatile!

1. To make the sauce, in a blender combine the avocado, Thai coconut flesh, water, lemon juice, raw honey, and sea salt; blend well.

2. To make the salad, grate the Granny Smith apples into a medium-size mixing bowl; add the goji berries and hemp seeds and toss to combine.

3. Add the sauce to the salad and toss to combine.

4. Chill in the refrigerator for about 1 hour before serving.

Note: This salad can be stored in the refrigerator for up to 4 days.

SPICY PESTO KALE SALAD

Basil and chipotle pepper provide a flavorful duo for a dish also rich in another twosome, vitamins A and B. Whether for dinner or lunch, as an entrée or a side, Spicy Pesto Kale Salad can add a savory zest to your daily menu.

1. To make the dressing, in a blender combine the olive oil, basil, chipotle pepper, sea salt, and garlic. Blend until well combined.

2. Add the pistachios and blend until rich and creamy.

3. To make the salad, in a medium-size mixing bowl, combine the kale, avocado, tomatoes, red bell pepper, and lemon juice.

4. Pour 4 to 6 tablespoons of the dressing over the salad and toss well to combine.

Note: The undressed salad can be stored in the refrigerator for up to 2 days and the dressing for up to 1 week. Add the dressing just before serving and toss to combine.

For the dressing:

1 cup extra-virgin olive oil

½ cup fresh basil

1 small dried chipotle pepper

1 teaspoon sea salt or dulse flakes

2 cloves garlic

¼ cup pistachios

For the salad:

4 cups chopped kale

1 Hass avocado, peeled, pitted, and chopped

2 Roma tomatoes, chopped

1 red bell pepper, stemmed, seeded, and chopped

Juice of 1 lemon

Makes 1 serving plus 2 dressing servings

For the filling:

2 cups finely chopped kale

1 cup diced cucumber

½ Hass avocado

1 mustard green leaf, chopped

1 tomato, diced (heirloom if possible for the delicious flavor!)

1 tablespoon 118 Spices*

1 tablespoon extra-virgin olive oil or flaxseed oil

For the sandwich:

2 slices sprouted grain bread or 2 slices Chia Buckwheat Bread (page 193)

⅓ cup Avocado Citrus Dressing (page 143)

Makes
1 sandwich

REGENERATION SALAD SANDWICH

Although regenerating cells is tough business, this recipe is rich in the greens and other ingredients needed to deliver oxygen and nutrients throughout the body. This sandwich is a fresh approach for supporting cellular regeneration, especially in your muscles and bones!

1. To make the filling, in a medium-size mixing bowl, toss together the kale, cucumber, avocado, mustard greens, tomato, spices, and oil until well combined.

2. To make the sandwich, place the bread on a flat surface. Spread with the Avocado Citrus Dressing and then evenly cover with the filling.

*A 118 Degrees restaurant favorite, this spice blend can be purchased through www.118degrees.com.

Note: This sandwich should be enjoyed fresh. The mixture, however, can be stored in the refrigerator for up to 1 day.

For the bowl:
2 cups chopped romaine lettuce

2 cups spinach

2 cups chopped kale

For the bruschetta:
4 Roma tomatoes, diced

½ cup chopped basil

3 cloves garlic, minced

1 teaspoon Himalayan salt

3 tablespoons dulse flakes

3 tablespoons hemp seeds

3 tablespoons capers

3 tablespoons extra-virgin olive oil

1 tablespoon lemon juice

Olives, spicy peppers, or avocado slices, for topping

Makes 2 entrée or 4 appetizer servings

BRUSCHETTA BOWL

A living-foods spin on a restaurant classic, this dish combines spices, superfoods, and sea vegetables. Enjoy this crisp, refreshing, and nutritionally powerful option as an entrée or a side dish.

1. To make the bowl, in a medium-size bowl, toss together the lettuce, spinach, and kale; separate into desired bowls to form the simple base of the dish.

2. To make the bruschetta, in a medium-size bowl, combine the tomatoes, basil, garlic, salt, dulse flakes, hemp seeds, capers, and olive oil, saving the lemon for last. Toss together well.

3. Divide evenly among the bowls. Add the topping of your choice.

Note: The bruschetta mixture can be stored in the refrigerator for up to 4 days.

ALMOND FIG SPREAD

Almonds and figs come together in this tasty spread that supports healthy bones. Enjoy on halved banana slices, on sprouted breads sprinkled with additional spices, or inside fresh peach halves warmed in the dehydrator.

....

1. In a food processor fitted with the S-blade, pulse the almonds until broken down into a meal. (If using raw almond butter, skip this step.) Add the figs, protein supplement, cinnamon, sea salt, and stevia.

2. Process until a rich spread has formed.

3. Transfer the mixture to an airtight container and refrigerate until ready to use. Use at room temperature for best results.

Note: This spread can be stored in the refrigerator for up to 10 days.

2 cups soaked almonds or raw almond butter

2 cups fresh or dried figs, reconstituted

½ cup protein supplement (hemp, brown rice, or pea protein)

2 teaspoons cinnamon

1 teaspoon sea salt

2 drops liquid stevia

Makes 4 cups

PUMPKIN SEED CHEESE

Ground seeds provide a nutritious basis for this colorful filler, topping, or spread. A nondairy staple in a raw-foods diet, Pumpkin Seed Cheese is superb for any use.

1 Roma tomato

¼ cup lemon juice

1 teaspoon sea salt

2 cloves garlic

4 cups pumpkin seeds

1. In a blender combine the tomato, lemon juice, sea salt, and garlic.

2. In a food processor fitted with the S-blade, pulse the pumpkin seeds into a fine meal. Add the blender mixture through the processor's chute and continue processing until well combined.

Note: The cheese can be stored in an airtight container in the pantry for up to 10 days.

Makes
3 cups

4 medium-size yams, cut into halves or quarters

4 cups water

1 tablespoon sea salt

For the marinade:
¼ cup extra-virgin olive oil

2 tablespoons chili powder

2 tablespoons dried onion

2 tablespoons nutritional yeast (optional)

1 tablespoon sea salt

Makes about 6 cups

YAM CHIPS

Yams are full of vitamin C, potassium, and iron. Enjoy these crunchy chips with a salad or as a stand-alone snack.

1. Prepare the yams by peeling the skins. (Because they do contain additional health benefits, if your preference is to use the skins, feel free.)

2. Using a food processor with the slicing blade, cut the yams into thin slices.*

3. In a medium-size mixing bowl, soak the yam slices in the water and sea salt for 4 to 6 hours.

4. Drain the yams completely and set aside.

5. To make the marinade, in a separate bowl, whisk together the olive oil, chili powder, dried onion, nutritional yeast, and sea salt.

6. Pour the marinade over the yams and toss well to coat.

7. Line 2 dehydrator trays with your choice of nonstick drying sheets.

8. Spread the yams evenly over the trays so that the pieces have little to no overlap.

9. Dehydrate at 118°F for 12 to 18 hours.

*A mandoline can be used to slice the yams into attractive rounds, but it takes longer than a food processor.

Note: The chips can be stored in an airtight container in the pantry indefinitely.

MINERAL MUSHROOM STEW

Cremini mushrooms, the lead ingredient in this dish, are a fantastic source of nutrition. When combined with other mushrooms, however, this stew sports all sorts of tastes and textures, making it a flavorful entrée adventure.

1. In a blender combine the squash and water with the kelp, miso, and garlic.

2. While still blending, add 2 cups of the cremini mushrooms and the ¼ cup of olive oil. Blend until well combined.

3. Add the remaining 2 cups cremini mushrooms and the shiitake and maitake mushrooms.

4. Pulse briefly until a stew-like consistency has formed.

5. Serve immediately or place in the dehydrator at 118°F for 1 hour before serving to create a rich flavor and thicker soup.

Note: This stew can be stored in the refrigerator for up to 5 days.

2 cups chopped yellow crookneck squash, plus ½ cup water or vegetable broth

2 tablespoons kelp granules

1 tablespoon miso paste

1 clove garlic

4 cups chopped cremini mushrooms

¼ cup extra-virgin olive oil

½ cup chopped shiitake mushrooms

½ cup chopped maitake mushrooms

Makes six 1-cup servings

For the greens mixture:

2 cups finely chopped kale

1 cup chopped mustard greens

1 cup red quinoa, steamed or sprouted*

1 tablespoon flaxseed oil

1 teaspoon 118 Spices** or spice blend of choice (page 23)

Juice of 1 lemon

For the veggie topping:

1 cup finely chopped red onion

1 cup diced tomato

½ cup finely grated carrot

½ Hass avocado, peeled, pitted, and diced

½ cup pumpkin seeds

⅓ cup diced mango

Makes 1 entrée or 2 appetizer servings

GORILLA BOWL

As humans, we can learn a few lessons from the dietary habits of our primate friends. If fruits and greens are good enough for the strongest animal in the jungle, they've surely got to be helpful in developing human strength. Introduce this lunch centerpiece to your children. It's a "Gorilla Bowl" of a meal.

1. To make the greens mixture, in a medium-size mixing bowl, combine the kale, mustard greens, red quinoa, flaxseed oil, 118 Spices, and lemon juice. Let stand so the kale can soften.

2. To make the veggie topping, in another mixing bowl, combine the red onion, tomato, carrot, avocado, pumpkin seeds, and mango.

3. Line 1 or 2 bowls with the greens mixture. Layer the veggie topping over the greens.

*To steam raw quinoa, place the quinoa in a steamer basket over a pot of water on the stove and steam for 7 minutes if presoaked and 15 minutes if not. To sprout, cover the quinoa with water and soak for 8 to 12 hours at room temperature. (You'll see tiny tails on the grains.) Rinse and then use.

**A 118 Degrees restaurant favorite, this spice can be purchased through www.118degrees.com.

Note: The salad can be stored in the refrigerator unassembled for up to 2 days.

ROOT VEGETABLE SOUFFLÉ

Prepare this dish at the beginning of the week, and dinner or lunch for more than one meal will be as close as your refrigerator. Root Vegetable Soufflé combines the colorful flavors of multiple vegetables with other nutrient-rich sources. Each serving is an energy builder that will also support your body.

....

1. To make the crust, in a food processor fitted with the S-blade, pulse the walnuts into a fine meal.

2. Add the Italian Blend seasoning and sea salt, and process again until a dough has formed.

3. Pat the dough into an 8 × 8-inch glass dish or onto a lined dehydrator tray, pressing into an 8 × 8-inch square.

4. To make the filling, place the butternut squash, tomato, water, red onion, garlic, and sea salt in a blender and blend until well combined.

5. Add the flaxseeds and blend until the mixture thickens.

6. Place the parsnips, carrots, and beets in a bowl and pour the mixture from the blender over the veggies. Toss together well.

7. Layer the mixture on the crust. If you are using a dehydrator, place the whole tray in the dehydrator and dehydrate at 118°F for 3 hours. Cut into squares and serve warm.

8. If you are not using a dehydrator, refrigerate the soufflé for 1 hour. Remove from the refrigerator, cut into squares, and let warm to room temperature before serving.

Note: This soufflé can be stored in the refrigerator for up to 4 days.

For the crust:
3 cups walnuts

2 tablespoons Italian Blend (page 23)

1 teaspoon sea salt or dulse flakes

For the filling:
2 cups diced butternut squash

1 Roma tomato or 1 red bell pepper, cored, seeded, and diced

1 cup water

¼ red onion

2 cloves garlic

1 teaspoon sea salt or dulse flakes

½ cup golden flaxseeds

2 cups shredded parsnip

2 cups shredded carrot

½ cup shredded beet

Makes
6 to 8
servings

2 large yams, peeled and diced*

For the sauce:
1 cup chopped zucchini

½ cup water

2 tablespoons yellow curry powder

2 tablespoons coconut oil

2 tablespoons raw honey or raw agave nectar

1 tablespoon white mellow miso paste (optional)

1 clove garlic

2 tablespoons ginger juice (sold as a liquid)

1 cup organic raisins, soaked in water and rinsed

Makes
2 entrée or
4 appetizer
portions

YAM CURRY BIRYANI

By combining lightly steamed yams with all the goodness of a raw topping, this transitional dish is designed specifically for people who aren't ready to move completely into living cuisine. It's a fantastic accompaniment for Sunday dinner or a holiday feast. If you're all-raw-all-the-time, however, just substitute yellow crookneck squash for the yams. Either way, it's a winner!

1. In a large ceramic stockpot over medium-high heat, steam the yams until tender, about 15 minutes. Remove and pat dry.

2. To make the sauce, in a blender combine the zucchini, water, yellow curry powder, coconut oil, raw honey, miso paste, garlic, and ginger juice until well blended. Pour the sauce over the yams. Sprinkle with the raisins and serve while still warm.

*If you're using yellow squash rather than yams, cube the squash and toss in the sauce. Let sit for 1 hour before sprinkling with the raisins and serving.

NORI ROLLS WITH TAHINI CRÈME

A quick and easy dish to prepare, these rolls are not only an ideal menu item for shortcut chefs but also a great way to alkalize the body. Nori is an important source of B vitamins and iron. Requiring no dehydration, these wraps are also gluten-free.

....

1. To make the crème, in a blender combine the tahini paste, lemon juice, cilantro, scallion, bell pepper, and garlic; pulse to a thick, paste-like crème.*

2. To make the wraps, on a cutting board, lay out the nori sheets.

3. Spread 2 tablespoons of the crème in the center of each sheet, horizontally.

4. Layer ½ cup each of baby kale and cucumber, followed by 2 slices each of avocado and jicama.

5. Roll the nori tightly, sealing with damp fingertips.

6. Repeat the process for the 3 remaining wraps. Serve immediately.

*Although a blender-created crème works beautifully for this recipe, the ingredients can be mixed in a food processor for a hummus-like spread.

For the crème:

1 cup raw tahini paste

⅓ cup lemon juice

2 tablespoons chopped cilantro

2 tablespoons chopped scallion

1 red bell pepper, stemmed, seeded, and chopped, or 1 Roma tomato, chopped

1 clove garlic

For the wrap:

4 raw nori sheets (I recommend Maine Coast Sea Vegetables.)

2 cups chopped baby kale

2 cups julienned cucumber

1 Hass avocado, quartered and cut into 8 pieces

8 sticks jicama

Makes
4 servings

6 cups pumpkin seeds,
plus extra for garnish

¾ cup raw cacao powder

1 tablespoon cinnamon

1 teaspoon sea salt

1 teaspoon nutmeg

½ cup raw agave nectar
or raw honey

Makes
sixteen
2 × 2-inch
bars

CACAO PUMPKIN SEED BARS

Cacao and pumpkin seeds combine in these divinely delicious snacks. They also contain a powerful mix of minerals—magnesium, phosphorous, potassium, and calcium—for your skeletal system. Enjoy between meals or as a healthy dessert.

1. In a food processor fitted with the S-blade, process the pumpkin seeds into a fine meal.

2. Add the cacao powder, cinnamon, sea salt, and nutmeg, and process until well combined.

3. Add the agave, drizzling it in from the top of the processor while it's still running; process until a dough ball has formed.

4. Line an 8 × 8-inch glass baking dish with parchment paper or wax paper and press the dough into the dish.

5. Top with additional pumpkin seeds for garnish and chill for ½ hour so the bars are easier to cut.

6. Cut into sixteen 2 × 2-inch bars and refrigerate.

Note: These bars can be stored in an airtight container in the pantry indefinitely. Cut them into fun shapes and wrap them individually for an easy grab-and-go snack.

A Final Note

Your musculoskeletal system—the bones, muscles, and connective tissue that give your body its unique form and function—must be strong to support and protect every part of your structure. But if you don't feed it properly, it can become damaged. A raw-food eating style is unique in that every item supplies your physical frame with essential nutrients. By eating a balanced diet of plant-based choices—starting with the recipes in this chapter—you *can* capture the vitamins, minerals, proteins/amino acids, and carbohydrates necessary to stay strong. The caveat is that to achieve optimal results, you'll likely have to supplement vitamin D or other nutrients not sufficiently available in your daily plan. In any case, a healthy musculoskeletal system is critical to your well-being and so is the target of Chapter 10, the enzymes of "Your Digestive Tract."

YOUR DIGESTIVE TRACT: ENZYMES TO THE RESCUE

If you're like me, you know the discomfort associated with digestive disorders. Ulcers, irritable bowel syndrome (IBS), gastroesophageal reflux disease (GERD), and similar conditions can wreak appetite-churning havoc with your system, destroying any interest you have in eating. They also can result from the body's inability to break down certain foods.

Your digestive tract is an amazing series of hollow organs—the mouth, esophagus, stomach, small and large intestines, rectum, and anus—drawn together by a tube that twists and turns from your mouth to the end of your colon. Digestion occurs as waves of muscle contractions propel food from organ to organ in what's known as peristalsis. Digestive juices produced along the way aid in pushing the food along and breaking it into nutrient molecules that can be absorbed easily. These juices are infused with enzymes, chemical catalysts that speed reactions throughout the body. With digestion, they not only help fragment every particle you eat but also extract the fats, proteins, carbohydrates, vitamins, salt, and water necessary to support function.

Although you're born with a bank of enzymes, you need additional supplies from your food choices to function optimally. Unfortunately, much of standard American dietary fare, such as meat, dairy, and heavily processed items, are devoid of sufficient enzymes. As such, they're not digested well. Instead, they can be as acidic or toxic to the digestive tract as they are to other parts of the body, causing inflammation and damage to the kidneys, gallbladder, liver, and other organs.

Living fruits, vegetables, nuts, seeds, and sprouted grains, however, are not only rich in their own vital nutrients but also contain the enzymes necessary to help your body in its food-breakdown-nutrient-assimilation tasks. In addition to naturally supporting digestion, they're alkaline, meaning they're more easily processed than other fare.

But of those foods, are some more effective than others? At least one leading naturopath believes the best way to achieve maximum results, through either a detox program or your daily consumption, is by weighting your diet toward as much fruit as possible. Why? Dr. Robert S. Morse, author of *The Detox Miracle Sourcebook*, suggests that in the evolutionary scheme of things, human beings were originally a subtropical species, genetically engineered as frugivores, or fruit eaters, rather than carnivores, or meat eaters, making a diet steeped in fruits a natural route to good health.

Moreover, berries, melons, and other fruits are not only enzyme abundant but also, as evidenced in Kirlian photography, electromagnetically charged. That is, they register the highest "energy algorithm of all foods," making them powerful *live* allies in reversing cellular decay while producing other health benefits for the body—including the digestive tract. "If you're trying to attain health, or remedy a problem," says Dr. Morse, "all raw fruit is your best bet because of its pure energy."

Most people would find the kind of fruitarian, or all-fruit, raw lifestyle that Dr. Morse has practiced personally for years too dramatic, let alone inconvenient. (A fruitarian diet is actually a vegan diet based on fruits, nuts, and seeds, with the addition of some vegetables, such as avocado and tomatoes, which are botanically classified as fruits.) Even Dr. Morse suggests introducing other plant-based items—veggies for rebuilding and herbs for regeneration—as part of his holistic approach for cleansing and restoring the body. His 70:30 or 80:20 ratio of raw to cooked foods might focus first on berries or melons for breakfast, followed by a salad for lunch and another salad and transitional foods—lightly steamed vegetables or a baked sweet potato—for dinner.

The raw-foods approach I promote in my books and at my 118 Degrees restaurants targets a mix of plant-based foods, including fresh fruits, melons, and berries, for their ability to alkalize the body, reduce inflammation, and stimulate self-healing. Whether fruits are the main focus or simply part of a balanced diet, they're essential in healing your digestive tract. You'll find it's easy to measure the incredible benefits of these health-stimulating foods once you start using them daily. By letting go of choices that are both acidic and too dense for your stomach and intestines—and embracing fresh, living options in their place—you'll feel revitalized. I promise!

I should know: Within just a few short weeks of switching from a standard American diet to fresh living foods, I found welcome relief from my many symptoms. Within one year, I was healed of my indigestion, heartburn, distended stomach, and cramping. For the first time in my adult life, I didn't experience low-level pain at every meal. I was restored, energized, and able to actually enjoy eating! I felt as if someone had given me the keys to the kingdom—that is, the kingdom of good health. It was an incredible "aha" moment that launched my passion for sharing this lifestyle with others.

A "Live" Solution

You'll see a reference throughout this chapter to probiotics. These are simply live bacteria much like the beneficial bacteria that already exist in your intestines. You may think it strange at first to consume bacteria, but your body uses friendly microbes all the time to assist with an array of functions. Your digestive tract, for instance, is home to an estimated 100 trillion microorganisms, belonging to various families.

Strains of certain bacteria, such as lactobacillus, not only assist in digestion and nutrient absorption but also keep harmful microbes in check so your intestines remain healthy. (Good bacteria are also believed to help support and facilitate the immune system.) Sometimes, however, infection, antibiotics, or other intestinal damage can throw the natural balance between "good" and "bad" bacteria off-kilter. That occurs when bad microbes are allowed to overgrow, leading to diarrhea and other digestive problems.

Researchers believe that the live enzyme–producing bacteria contained in probiotics can restore the system's normal flora and, in the process, improve intestinal function. Studies have shown that as a healthy counterpoint to the "bad" bacteria in your system, probiotics can help address several gastrointestinal conditions. For instance, a 2011 Yale University School of Medicine panel concluded from a review of current research that probiotics can be effective in preventing antibiotic-related and infectious diarrhea. They can also aid in treating ulcerative colitis and childhood diarrhea, in addition to supporting or boosting the immune system. Probiotics also may be beneficial for irritable bowel syndrome, vaginitis, and diarrhea and Crohn's disease linked to *Clostridium difficile* bacteria, although the evidence, according to the ten-expert panel, is less convincing and needs more study.

Probiotic Supplements

Whatever your condition, the good news is that probiotics are readily available in dietary supplements (powders, tablets, capsules, and concentrated liquids), which can be easily added to foods or taken directly. To produce the supplements, the microorganisms are cultured in a lab and freeze-dried before being compacted into easily digested and absorbed delivery systems. They usually need to be refrigerated to maintain their strength.

Whatever the form, as long as the supplement contains enough living organisms to grow in your intestines, you'll likely experience the benefits. Recommended dosages are measured in colony-forming units, or CFUs, microscopic units ranging from millions to billions. Maintaining a healthy intestinal flora requires two or more billion live cells, taken either daily or several days a week. Up to ten billion cultures may be necessary to address a specific imbalance.

Here's a caveat to remember: The Food and Drug Administration currently doesn't regulate probiotics like it does drugs, so supplements can vary in potency and quality. You'll want to check with your physician or natural-health provider as to the correct product, dosage, and usage. Because studies have shown that different bacterial strains provide different benefits, targeting the best options will help you attain optimal results. Also, although probiotics are generally safe, effective, and easily tolerated, a health practitioner can guide you as to the appropriateness of using a supplement, depending on your overall health.

Fermented Foods

Besides probiotic supplements, you also can capture the positive effects of friendly microorganisms from fermented foods—foods that are preserved either naturally or by processing with good microbes as the preservative agent.

Fermented foods have played an important role in the diets of many cultures over the centuries. By replenishing naturally beneficial flora in the body, especially the digestive tract, they, too, fight off and prevent the growth of unhealthy or destructive bacteria and other unfriendly substances. In so doing, fermented foods not only help keep your system in balance but are also believed to aid in releasing nutrients, increasing enzymes, and making foods easier to digest.

If you're eating a traditional diet, your likely probiotic or fermented choices include yogurt and other cultured dairy products. But with a raw diet, you'll need to incorporate different types of selections to introduce indigenous or naturally friendly bacteria into your body. Luckily there are abundant food and drink options that you can either purchase at a health food store or ferment at home to satisfy those needs. Sauerkraut, miso, and a Korean veggie staple known as kimchi (or kimchee) top a fermented-food list that also includes probiotic beverages such as coconut kefir (fermented coconut water) and kombucha (an ancient Chinese tea known for more than 250 years for its digestive properties). Whatever you choose, by adding a "live solution" to your diet, you're balancing your inner ecosystem.

For the brine:
1 quart water

2 tablespoons sea salt

For the veggie mix:
1 head cabbage

1 cucumber

Vegetables of choice, such as a carrot or red or green bell pepper

Makes
1 quart

FERMENTED SAUERKRAUT

If you're so inclined, you can ferment foods in your own kitchen using a simple process. Sauerkraut is a good first attempt because it involves produce you likely have on hand.

1. To make the brine, combine the water and salt in a bowl and mix until the salt dissolves.

2. To make the veggie mix, chop the cabbage, cucumber, and other vegetables.

3. Place the vegetables in a 1-quart glass jar and push to the bottom.

4. Cover with the brine.

5. Seal the jar, placing a heavy object on top of the cover to hold it in place as gases collect. Place in a bowl on your countertop.

6. Open once a day to let any gases escape.

7. After 3 days, your veggies should be ready to enjoy. They can be refrigerated indefinitely.

A Cleansing Ritual

Many people dive into living cuisine through the Three-Day Jump Start I introduced in Chapter 3. By incorporating raw foods and eating habits into their daily routine, they get a quick taste of a new lifestyle. But there's another way to achieve a healthy jolt to your digestive and other systems. Detoxification is an intense weeklong or multiweek process of breaking decisively with your old diet and ushering in your new one. (Think of it as "cold turkey"!)

The concept of cleansing the body in an effort to spark renewed strength and vitality is as old as the fasting traditions of the early Christian church and as widespread as the world's greatest cultures. Clearing your digestive tract of the acidic spin-offs of processed foods, sugars, dairy, and meats can be a key first step in transitioning to raw foods. In terms of living cuisine, the process involves a stringent protocol of healthy food choices—leafy green vegetables, fresh fruits, and water, plus some lean proteins—and holistic lifestyle changes to synergistically support your body, mind, and spirit.

By cleaning out harmful toxins in favor of healthy substitutes, a detox stimulates healing and a shift toward overall good health. Not only does it make way for enzymes and nutrients—the "good stuff"—to restore your physique, but it also prompts the release of all sorts of toxins in your life. It's as important to cleanse your mind and your surroundings as it is to physically purge your body. Filling your space with positive people, thoughts, and activities (affirmations, stretching, and other exercise) is the only way to support your growth.

Is detoxing necessary for everyone? No. Some people can ease into a raw-foods diet very successfully without detoxification as a pathway. In either case, cleansing provides a clean break with your old eating style and a quick way to clear your digestive tract and other systems of stored toxins, and it complements your new eating plan.

Because there are many variations on the detox theme, you may want to consult an integrative-health professional to individualize one to your particular needs. (As with any dramatic dietary change, discuss this approach with your physician, especially if you're suffering from a major health issue.) A practitioner will assess your health goals and any preexisting conditions before creating a diet and detox plan unique to you. That might involve adding probiotics and supplements or just sticking with low-glycemic fruits and grains. Although a 7-day detox is a fantastic start, 21 to 28 days is optimal. Some people divide the time into a week each of cooked vegan foods, raw foods, and liquids, finishing the cycle with a fourth or final week of raw foods. Others combine an all-raw diet with herbal cleanses.

Whatever path you choose, you may feel uncomfortable at first. But I urge you to be diligent. One intense detox week can be a powerful quick-start to a healthy, holistic lifestyle. Two to three weeks can recalibrate your system even more effectively. It can return you to your natural state of homeostasis, or balance, in a quicker fashion than just easing into living foods. In the meantime, even without a structured detox program, you can help yourself immensely by eliminating the physical and emotional toxins that impede your progress and replacing them with choices that bolster body, mind, and soul.

Advice from the Chef

To optimize digestion:

- Target your daily menu with foods known for their anti-inflammatory abilities. Enzyme- and nutrient-filled greens and sea vegetables optimize the digestive tract by cleansing and fortifying. Aloe vera supplements can also be helpful.

- Drink your greens! An alkalizing smoothie can reduce stress and restore balance after a digestive attack.

- Enjoy one type of nut or seed per dish for optimal digestion. For additional flavoring, pulverize and blend almonds into crèmes, sauces, and beverages, which are easier to digest than crunching the whole nut. Also, tread lightly with fat-rich cashews because they can inflame the body.

- Incorporate probiotics and probiotic beverages as digestive aids. They can help flush your system of unwelcome toxins.

- Select yeast-free foods when possible. Vegetables, whole grains, and beans reduce the risk of yeast infections, particularly Candida albicans. Although these harmless bacteria exist in every body, they thrive on the yeast found in certain sugar-filled and fermented foods. Overgrowth can lead to myriad health problems, including digestive issues. Although fruits can be yeast instigators, they're still important for their nutrient and other digestive plusses. Balance in all things.

Affirmations
for Digestive Health

Oprah Winfrey is well-known for both her media genius and the personal connection she has with viewers. One advice gem from the maven of talk: "Learn to let your intuition—gut instinct—tell you when the food, the relationship, the job isn't good for you and, conversely, when what you're doing is just right." I'd say touché, and add these other affirmation jewels for your digestive tract:

- *To address heartburn:* "I breathe freely and fully. I am safe. I trust the process of life."

- *To counter an ulcer, IBS, or GERD:* "As I release the past, the new, fresh, and vital enter. I allow life to flow through me."

GINGER JUICE COCKTAIL

A well-known digestive aid, ginger juice helps flush the body of toxins. But it also keeps you warm in the winter. Depending on the season, enjoy this cocktail either warm or cold.

2 fresh pears

1 cup grapes with seeds

¼ cup grated ginger

1 teaspoon cinnamon

1. Press the pears, grapes, and ginger through a juicer.

2. Transfer the juice to a blender; blend in the cinnamon.

Note: This cocktail can be stored in the refrigerator for up to 2 days.

Makes
1 serving

4 cups diced cantaloupe

2 cups fresh coconut water

6 tablespoons white chia seeds

Fresh mint leaves, for garnish

Makes two
16-ounce
servings

CANTALOUPE AND WHITE CHIA TONIC

For a great morning boost, try this simple tonic. It combines melons and chia seeds, ingredients known for aiding digestion. Keep it on your menu, especially during summer's peak melon season. Also, don't be afraid to experiment with honeydew and other melon favorites.

1. In a blender combine the cantaloupe with the coconut water until a thick puree is formed.

2. Toss in the chia seeds and let stand for 5 minutes.

3. Blend or stir the contents vigorously before pouring into glasses; garnish with a mint leaf. Enjoy immediately.

Note: The chia seeds will naturally become sticky, creating a fun texture to enjoy with your life-giving tonic blend.

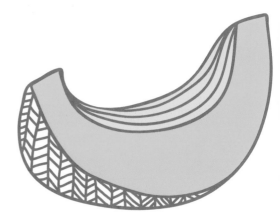

CHIA BUCKWHEAT BREAD

Soft yet sturdy, this bread is a great high-protein, gluten-free option that blends sprouted grains with chia seeds, which are rich in calcium and essential fatty acids. One 4-ounce serving contains more than 9 grams of protein as well as your daily requirement for omega-3s.

1. In a food processor fitted with the S-blade, pulse the buckwheat until ground into a fine meal.

2. Add the chia seeds and tomatoes, processing the ingredients again into a rough mixture.

3. Add the water, olive oil, chili powder, garlic, and sea salt, processing until a dough-like mixture has formed.

4. Line a dehydrator tray with your choice of nonstick drying sheet.

5. Gently press the mixture onto the tray to a thickness of no more than ¼ inch. (You may elect to do 2 trays of thinner bread.)

6. Dehydrate the bread at 115°F for 6 hours. After 3 hours, flip the bread directly onto the screen, removing the nonstick drying sheet.

*To sprout raw buckwheat, cover the grains with water and soak for 8 to 12 hours at room temperature. (You'll see tiny tails on the grains.) Rinse and then use.

Note: This bread can be stored in the refrigerator for up to 2 weeks.

4 cups buckwheat, sprouted*

½ cup chia seeds

2 Roma tomatoes

½ cup water

2 tablespoons extra-virgin olive oil

1 tablespoon chili powder

2 cloves garlic

1 teaspoon sea salt

Makes 16 slices

For the salad:

6 cups mixed berries

2 tablespoons coconut oil

2 cups diced pears

2 tablespoons orange zest

For the dressing:

½ Hass avocado, peeled and pitted

½ cup coconut water

¼ cup orange juice

1 tablespoon raw honey

Makes
4 servings

PEAR BERRY SALAD

This dish can be prepared using any type of berries, including huckleberries. Choose fruits that are local and in season for a salad that truly shines.

1. To make the salad, rinse the berries well; combine in a medium-size mixing bowl with the coconut oil and toss until well coated. Add the pears and orange zest and toss again.

2. Chill the salad while preparing the dressing.

3. To make the dressing, in a blender combine the avocado, coconut water, orange juice, and raw honey and blend well. (You can also use an immersion blender for this task.)

4. Line each bowl for serving with ¼ cup of the dressing, top with 2 cups of the salad mixture, and enjoy!

Note: This salad can be stored in the refrigerator for up to 3 days.

BABY KALE SALAD WITH SPANISH GARDEN DRESSING

Baby kale, a sweeter but nutrient-dense version of the more typical lacinato, or curly kale, forms the basis for a luncheon salad that's topped with a tasty dressing. What's fun about this dish—other than simply eating it—is that you can harvest your own kale from ancient heirloom seeds. Just place them in a backyard planter or a vertical garden. You'll have greens for a salad in just 3 to 4 weeks.

....

1. To make the dressing, in a food processor fitted with the S-blade, combine the tomatoes, onion, avocado oil, cilantro, garlic, lime juice, and chili powder. Pulse into a salsa-like mixture. (It should not be pureed.)

2. To make the salad, in a large mixing bowl, combine the kale, broccoli, dulse, tomato, cucumber, pumpkin seeds, and avocado.

3. Drizzle with the dressing, toss until well blended, and serve.

For the dressing:

2 Roma tomatoes, diced

½ cup chopped yellow or red onion

¼ cup avocado oil, hemp oil, or olive oil

¼ cup fresh cilantro, leaves only

2 tablespoons chopped garlic

2 tablespoons lime juice

2 tablespoons chili powder

For the salad:

6 cups baby kale leaves

2 cups chopped broccoli

2 cups dulse leaves, pulled apart

1 cup diced tomato

1 cup diced cucumber (with skin)

1 cup pumpkin seeds

1 Hass avocado, peeled, pitted, and diced

Makes
2 entrée or
4 appetizer
servings

2 cups celery juice or vegetable broth*

2 tablespoons ginger juice (optional)

¼ cup flaxseed oil or olive oil

2 carrots, diced

½ cup chopped butternut squash

2 tablespoons earth mineral supplement, miso paste, or liquid trace minerals

2 tablespoons kelp granules

1 tablespoon chili powder

1 teaspoon sea salt

1 clove garlic

Makes
4 servings

EARTH SOUP

Composed of root vegetables and a blend of spices, this lunch or dinner entrée strengthens and supports optimal digestion via the many vitamins and minerals that come together in this delicious soup. The addition of trace mineral supplements to the carrots, squash, and other spices intensifies the overall nutritious effects.

1. Combine the celery juice, ginger juice, and oil in a blender and emulsify until slightly warm.

2. Add the carrots, squash, mineral supplement, kelp granules, chili powder, sea salt, and garlic. Blend and enjoy.

*It's best to enjoy this soup at room temperature or up to 118°F. To enjoy it warm, heat the juice in a stockpot on the stove before blending.

Note: This soup can be stored in the refrigerator for up to 3 days.

2 cups chopped collard greens

2 cups chopped kale

2 cups chopped Swiss chard, spinach, or bok choy

½ cup chopped mustard greens

2 tablespoons lemon juice

1 teaspoon sea salt or dulse flakes

¼ cup flaxseed oil or hemp oil

3 cloves garlic, minced

Makes
5 cups

SAVORY GARLIC GREENS

Just as the name implies, Savory Garlic Greens is a tasty, healthy living-foods option. It's replete with not only essential vitamins and minerals but also the enzymes necessary for digestive efficiency. With the addition of flaxseed oil or hemp oil in the dressing, this dish is also rich in omega-3 fatty acids. Mix and serve immediately as an entrée or a side.

1. Combine the collard greens, kale, Swiss chard, and mustard greens in a medium-size mixing bowl.

2. Add the lemon juice and sea salt, and toss to combine.

3. In a separate bowl, whisk together the flaxseed oil and garlic.

4. Add to the greens and toss until the leaves are completely coated.

Note: Use this recipe as a base for additional items, such as avocados, olives, and walnuts. The mixture can be stored in the refrigerator for up to 4 days.

RAINBOW WRAPS

Raw nori sheets or a light piece of chard form the basis for this sandwich. The filling provides a full spectrum of vitamins and minerals in a delicious and vibrant presentation.

....

1. To make the sauce, whisk together the coconut water, scallion, coconut aminos, lime juice, and Thai chili pepper.

2. To make the filling, in a medium-size mixing bowl, combine the mango, carrot, green papaya, and sunflower sprouts. Add the sauce, tossing well until the vegetables are coated.

3. To create the wraps, lay the Swiss chard leaves on a cutting board.

4. Divide the filling evenly among the wraps, making sure the mango slices are placed lengthwise.

5. Roll tightly. For the chard wraps, close each with a toothpick. For the nori wraps, use a small amount of water to seal the edges. Chill for 1 hour and then serve.

Note: These wraps can be stored in the refrigerator for up to 2 days.

6 Swiss chard leaves or raw nori wraps

For the sauce:
⅓ cup coconut water

⅓ cup chopped scallion

¼ cup coconut aminos

2 tablespoons lime juice

1 Thai chili pepper, diced, or 1 tablespoon Thai chili paste

For the filling:
2 cups sliced mango

2 cups shredded carrot

2 cups shredded green papaya

2 cups sunflower sprouts

Makes
4 to 6
servings

DULCE DE LECHE PINEAPPLE

The fruit that stars in this dish produces more than a fresh taste for breakfast or dessert. Rich in nutrients, pineapple also contains bromelain, an enzyme important in digestion. A sauce of coconut, cinnamon, and nutmeg offers additional antioxidant boosters and flavor to the mix.

1. For best sauce results, use an immersion blender to combine the sweetener, maca root, coconut butter, cinnamon, nutmeg, and sea salt. Otherwise, whisk the ingredients in a bowl until well blended.

2. Add the pineapple to a medium-size bowl, pour on the sauce, and toss to combine.

3. Chill in the refrigerator until ready to serve. Just before serving, sprinkle with the shredded coconut.

Note: This dish can be stored in the refrigerator for up to 4 days. Dulce de Leche Pineapple may also be made into a dried fruit snack for a longer shelf life. Just dehydrate the mixture on a nonstick drying tray at 118°F for 12 hours.

4 cups diced pineapple

For the sauce:
¼ cup liquid sweetener of choice (coconut nectar, raw honey, or yacon syrup)

2 tablespoons maca root

1 tablespoon coconut butter (optional)

1 tablespoon cinnamon

1 teaspoon nutmeg

½ teaspoon sea salt

½ cup shredded coconut, for garnish

Makes
4 cups

A Final Note

Your digestive tract feels like the center of the universe, especially when it's in distress. A variety of disorders can cause gas, bloating, and other serious symptoms that ruin your appetite and put you generally out of sorts. The fruits, vegetables, and other options in a plant-based diet, however, can keep your digestive tract healthy and functioning smoothly. They do so, in part, by providing extra enzymes to help facilitate the breakdown of food into easily absorbed nutrient molecules. In addition to enzymes, your digestive tract can also benefit from probiotics, "friendly" bacteria that, when introduced through supplements or fermented foods, can be a force in correcting an ecosystem out of whack. So if a living-foods diet can help your digestive tract, what else can it do? Chapter 11, "Healthy Children, Healthy Families," takes a look.

PART THREE

Healing

THE WHOLE

HEALTHY CHILDREN, HEALTHY FAMILIES

Growing a healthy family begins at the end of a fork. With childhood obesity the number one pediatric health issue in the U.S., it's important for young children and teens to eat nutritiously. What you serve at the dinner table has profound implications for a lifetime! Unfortunately, some of the most commonplace toxins to a growing body appear in the most popular of childhood foods—candy, cookies, cakes, sodas, and other junk-food items. But any food processed from refined sugar, refined flour, dairy products, or genetically modified oils can contribute to food allergies, digestive distress, acne, or attention deficit disorders. Studies have consistently shown that overweight children with poor eating habits are at risk now and later for type 2 diabetes and a raft of other chronic health issues—asthma, high cholesterol, heart disease, and even some cancers.

The ABCs of Eating Raw

Getting rid of empty calories and saturated or unhealthy fats can indeed help your child maintain an optimal weight, the first prerequisite of a strong and fit body. But trading the toxins—artificial sweeteners, food colorings, sugar, cow's milk, and gluten sources—in processed foods for a more natural path achieves more than weight goals.

Plant-based foods also provide the nutrient building-blocks children and adolescents need to facilitate bone growth and strength, produce red blood cells, boost the immune system, generate energy, and encourage every other job in a developing body. Organic and pesticide-free fruits and vegetables, along with nuts, seeds, and healthy grains, supply unadulterated vitamins, minerals, whole proteins, complex carbohydrates, healthy fats, fiber, and living enzymes necessary for function and growth. They also create an environment that supports health, not disease.

"An alkaline balanced body," says Michael W. Shannon, a Laguna Hills, California, pediatrician and longtime advocate of a plant-based diet as a nutrition option for children, "is just as important in children as it is in adults to prevent the health consequences of acidity."

The key in retrieving these multiple nutrients, however, is to include a large variety of raw and lightly cooked foods (prepared using healthy techniques, if desired) throughout the week so your child reaps the wellness rewards of a balanced diet. In terms of pediatric health, your selections should target:

- Fresh vegetables such as yams, broccoli, and dark leafy greens
- Fresh fruits such as pears, blueberries, and apples
- Water—every child needs it for growth and development

In terms of foods for specific stages of growth and development, Dr. Shannon suggests avocado in infancy, nut butters in childhood, and nuts and seeds in adolescence. Yes, you can use a raw-foods approach with babies because their diet already consists primarily of fruits and veggies in addition to breast milk. My children have been raw foodies *and* healthy since infancy! There is a caveat, however. Even though a raw-foods diet is a viable option for children, you need to carefully monitor their intake of vitamins, minerals, essential fatty acids, protein, and other nutrients. Because living cuisine contains no cow's milk, for instance, it's important to tap other bountiful sources of certain nutrients. Also, fruits and vegetables contain sufficient calcium, but your child will likely need a vitamin D supplement.

Also, just as it's important for you to talk to your physician about *your* diet, it's critical to let your pediatrician know what your child is eating. A health practitioner can not only ensure that his or her nutritional requirements are being met but also alert you to any potential deficiencies based on blood work. I encourage you to find a medical professional aligned with your value system regarding food so you can be true partners in your child's optimal health.

Also, be willing to stay the course. Eating raw as a family requires an effort that not every parent is willing to make, even though it can be nutritionally beneficial. To give your children sufficient "good stuff," especially from vegetables, you'll need to creatively incorporate options such as green smoothies, zucchini pastas, and fruit-based desserts. Moreover, you'll want to be sure that you're buying only fresh organics as often as possible because the growing process hasn't depleted these foods of magnesium and other nutrients important for growth and development. They're also not contaminated with pesticides and other allergens that might trigger food allergies.

Do you have to start with 100 percent raw? No. A diet that's 50 percent living foods is a good beginning threshold. Whatever approach you choose, however, learn as much as possible about the nuances of balancing protein, carbohydrates, and fat along with maintaining adequate minerals and vitamins. Also stay abreast of the latest findings. As research continues into the viability of a raw-foods diet, you'll want the latest information so you can make the best choices for your family. "Going slowly and getting educated," says Dr. Shannon, "is a good direction for families to take initially."

Making It Fun

Even if *you're* a dedicated raw foodie, you might find it difficult to motivate your children to follow suit, unless, of course, they've been raised on this path. Children can be habitual eaters, so suggesting something out of the blue and expecting a receptive response might be a challenge. But by introducing tasty living-cuisine items in small, fun ways, you can cultivate healthy habits in them.

- *First*, grow an herb garden or a full-fledged garden together. "Farming" with your child will help you connect the idea of organic vegetables and healthy eating.

- *Second*, shop and prepare foods as a team. The joy of empowering my children with healthy options by doing these two tasks with them far exceeds the time and dedication it takes to make it work! For a quick and easy start, add items for a smoothie to your shopping list. When you get home, set up your blender or juicer so your child can make a drink from the apples, cantaloupe, citrus fruits, or berries you've just purchased. Other flavorings to include are almond butter, bananas, cacao, and goji berries, to name a few. Keep the final ingredients to three colorful choices so your finished drink has kid eye appeal.

- *Third*, adapt your raw-food dishes to your child's palate and developmental needs. Be flexible. If he or she doesn't like the texture of leafy greens, for instance, puree them for a soup or sauce or sneak them into a fruit-based smoothie. If you're concerned that nuts are a choking hazard, grind them for a nut butter or shake.

- *Fourth*, pack and pair. Although a raw-foods diet is about healthy alternatives, it also needs to be interesting. Pack a picnic of your child's colorful favorites and a few new snack options and head off to the park, swimming pool, or zoo. Pairing tasty food with a favorite adventure can leave a positive, lasting impression of both the experience and the cuisine!

Advice from the Chef

To strengthen the family:

- Go on the offensive. Line your kitchen counters and pantry shelves with healthy snacks. It's the best way to direct your children toward quality foundational living foods.

- Stock your cupboards with brain-building essential fats—coconut butter, almond butter, hemp seeds, pumpkin seeds, and avocados. They'll enhance any basic dish.

- Plant your child's favorite fresh herb in a kitchen garden and think of ways to use it. Children love what they learn to love, and introducing them to new flavors as you cook will encourage explorations of all sorts. Try mint, for instance, as a garnish.

- Make family meals a buffet of raw-food tacos, salads, and even pasta dishes. Your children will enjoy the casualness while you can tailor selections to satisfy multiple ages, growth spurts, and palates.

- Pack raw-food desserts with ingredients that might otherwise be challenging for your children to love and eat. Although desserts in this diet are often packed with protein from crushed nuts and seeds, hiding a little spirulina within the sweets adds to the mix.

Affirmations
for the Family

Getting your children to eat properly can be a daily hassle. It takes time, patience, and sometimes a little strong-arming to make kids eat what's good for them, rather than what appeals to their sugar instincts. But by introducing healthier choices early in their lives, you help your cause. Try these affirmations to keep the benefits in your mind's eye.

- "My children are developing healthy bodies from excellent sources of nutrition."

- "My family's nutritional needs are being fully met by a clean, whole-foods diet."

FAMILY FIVE SMOOTHIE

The family version of a popular recipe in my book *Raw Basics,* this smoothie provides a balanced nutritional meal in a cup: fresh fruit, greens, essential fatty acids, superfoods, plus a sweetener. Packed with protein, vitamins, and minerals, this version is easy for any young chef to create.

1. In a blender combine all the ingredients until smooth.

2. Pack into airtight containers for lunch on the go or serve in a bowl to accompany your favorite entrée.

Note: You may wish to freeze the banana in advance for a chilled smoothie, or try ice if you like frosty smoothies.

1 banana

1 cup fresh spinach leaves

1 cup diced mango or pineapple

1 cup water, Almond Shortcut Milk (page 42), or coconut milk

2 tablespoons coconut butter or almond butter

2 tablespoons hemp seeds or hemp protein

Makes
two 10-ounce
servings

For the crust:

4 cups walnuts or pecans

⅔ cup yacon syrup or coconut nectar

2 tablespoons orange juice

For the topping:

2 Hass avocados, peeled and pitted

⅓ cup coconut butter

1½ cups fresh orange juice

½ cup orange slices

Makes sixteen 2 × 2-inch bars

CITRUS AVOCADO BARS

Incorporating nuts, avocado, fresh oranges, and coconut butter, this recipe is a tasty way to increase the nutrient building blocks your children need for a strong body. They're simple to make and fun to eat!

1. To make the crust, in a food processor fitted with the S-blade, pulse the walnuts into a fine meal.

2. Add the yacon syrup and orange juice and process until a dough-like mixture has formed.

3. Pat the crust into an 8 × 8-inch glass dish.

4. To make the topping, place the avocados, coconut butter, orange juice, and orange slices in a blender and blend until well combined.

5. Spread the topping over the crust and freeze for 1 hour to set. Cut into sixteen 2 × 2-inch bars.

Note: These bars can be stored in the refrigerator for up to 1 week.

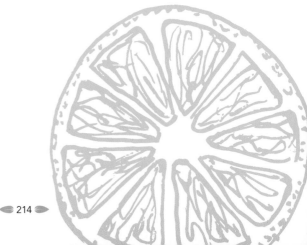

NUT BUTTER BITES

The essential fatty acids and other nutrients in this treat can have positive effects throughout your body, especially in building healthy brain tissue. With the addition of the nut butters, these bites are also great for pregnant and breast-feeding women who need more healthy fats.

....

1. In a medium-size mixing bowl, combine the nut butter, hemp protein, yacon syrup, cinnamon, and sea salt. Using a spatula, stir the ingredients together until well combined.

2. Add the buckwheat and continue stirring until a large ball has formed.

3. Pat the mixture into an 8 × 8-inch glass dish or onto a tray and flatten into an 8 × 8-inch square. Cut into sixteen 2 × 2-inch squares.**

4. Refrigerate until ready to enjoy.

*To sprout raw buckwheat, cover the grains with water and soak for 8 to 12 hours at room temperature. (You'll see tiny tails on the grains.) Rinse and then use.

**For a variation on the squares, cut the dough into rounds using either a 2-inch-diameter cookie cutter or the top of a juice glass.

Note: These bites can be stored in the refrigerator for up to 1 week.

1 cup almond butter or other nut butter

½ cup hemp protein

¼ cup yacon syrup or 3 drops liquid stevia

1 tablespoon cinnamon

1 teaspoon sea salt

1 cup buckwheat, sprouted*

Makes sixteen 2 × 2-inch bars

4 cups red walnut pieces

2 cups pitted dates

1 teaspoon cinnamon

1 teaspoon sea salt

Makes
24 snacks

RED WALNUT AND DATE SNACKS

A colorful option that can be stored on the countertop, this snack taps red walnuts, a staple from the produce section at your health food store.

1. In a food processor fitted with the S-blade, lightly pulse together all the ingredients.

2. When the mixture begins to stick to itself, remove and transfer to a small bowl.

3. Using a tablespoon, scoop out 2 tablespoons of the dough mixture at a time.

4. Roll into a ball and place in candy cups. Keep on the counter!

Note: Regular walnuts can be substituted for red walnuts. Also add ½ cup of goji berries for color and extra nutritional value.

4 cups quinoa, soaked
in water to cover and
drained*

1 cup water

1 tablespoon sea salt

1 Roma tomato or red
bell pepper, stemmed,
seeded, and cored

¼ cup seasoning of
choice (I like both chili
powder and the Italian
Blend, page 23.)

4 cups flaxseeds, soaked
in water to cover and
drained**

6 tablespoons dulse
flakes

Makes
sixteen
4 × 4-inch
crackers

FLAX QUINOA CRACKERS

A crispy snack for kids of all ages, these crackers are high
in protein, one of the body's essential building blocks.
In addition to a spectrum of important minerals, this recipe offers an infusion of omega-3 fatty acids, which are
necessary for boosting brainpower and other essential
functions.

1. Combine the quinoa, water, sea salt, tomato, and seasoning in a blender. Blend well until a thick puree has
formed.

2. Place the flaxseeds in a large bowl, add the quinoa puree, and stir until well combined.

3. Line 4 dehydrator trays with nonstick sheets. Spread
the mixture evenly over all 4 trays, creating a thin layer
of cracker.

4. Sprinkle the dulse flakes over each tray before placing
it in the dehydrator. Dehydrate on 118°F for 12 hours, or
until completely crunchy.

5. Remove the sheets from the dehydrator tray by invert-
ing them onto a cutting board. Cut evenly across both
directions to create 4 × 4-inch squares.

*Quinoa will sprout in as few as 6 hours. Place in a bowl and cover
with water, with an extra inch of water on top. Leave on the counter
for 6 hours. Rinse and drain before use.

**Flaxseed becomes very sticky when soaked. After soaking with
water to cover the flaxseeds for at least 1 hour, combine the ge-
latinous mixture straight into the recipe.

Note: These crackers can be stored in an airtight container in the
pantry indefinitely.

SWEET ALMOND SOUP

Kids love rich, creamy soups, and this one has proven a winner in our house. While the zucchini, flaxseed, and almonds help alkalize the body and tend to the development needs of the brain and other systems, the honey and chili powder add a mix of flavors that prompts my family to ask for Sweet Almond Soup.

1. In a blender combine the celery, zucchini, hot water, flaxseed oil, raw honey, chili powder, and garlic. Blend until well combined.

2. Add the almonds and blend on high for about 2 minutes, until a rich and thick soup has formed.

*In living-cuisine prep, 100° to 110°F constitutes "hot"; 80° to 100°F constitutes "lukewarm." Temperatures can be measured easily with a standard candy thermometer.

Note: Great alone or as an accompaniment for a salad, Sweet Almond Soup can be stored in the refrigerator for up to 3 days and then gently warmed in the blender or on the stove top.

2 stalks celery

1 small zucchini

3 cups hot water*

¼ cup flaxseed oil or coconut oil

2 tablespoons raw honey or raw agave nectar or 2 drops liquid stevia

1 tablespoon mild chili powder

½ clove garlic

1 cup almonds

Makes
4 servings

FUSION PASTA

A departure from the gluten-filled noodles in a tradition-al diet, these squash noodles are a fun, nutritious option for kids. Although you can modify the veggie toppings to suit your family's preferences, this recipe calls for a basic red sauce that most kids will enjoy.

....

1. To make the pasta, slice the zucchini lengthwise using the julienne blade of a mandoline.* Place in a medium-size bowl.

2. Add the carrot, dates, spinach, quinoa, and hemp seeds to the squash noodles and toss to combine.

3. To make the sauce, in a blender combine the sun-dried tomatoes, olive oil, raw honey, basil, Roma tomatoes, and garlic, and blend until a thick puree has formed.

4. To serve immediately, whisk ½ cup hot water into the sauce, toss with the noodles, divide among 4 plates, and serve warm. To keep warm while you're preparing other dishes for your meal, mix the sauce and noodles togeth-er, divide among 4 plates, and place in the dehydrator at 118°F.

*An OXO Good Grips mandoline works well for this recipe.

Note: This dish can be stored in the refrigerator for up to 2 days. Water separation is natural, so drain the pasta before serving.

For the pasta:
2 large zucchini or 4 small yellow crookneck squash

1 cup shredded carrot

1 cup diced dates

1 cup finely chopped spinach

1 cup quinoa (optional, for additional protein)

¼ cup hemp seeds or ⅓ cup pine nuts

For the sauce:
1 cup sun-dried tomatoes

3 tablespoons extra-virgin olive oil

2 tablespoons raw honey or raw agave nectar

4 fresh basil leaves

2 Roma tomatoes

½ clove garlic

½ cup hot water

Makes
4 servings

2 cups pumpkin seeds

1 cup diced tomato

3 tablespoons lemon juice

3 tablespoons diced scallion

1 clove garlic

1 tablespoon sea salt

4 tablespoons golden flaxseed meal

2 cups quinoa, sprouted*

Makes twelve 1-inch falafel

PUMPKIN AND QUINOA FALAFEL

My adaptation of a traditional crispy Middle Eastern food, this falafel serves as a great stand-alone snack, sandwich, or salad topping. Use your dehydrator to create the familiar falafel texture.

1. In a food processor fitted with the S-blade, process the pumpkin seeds into a fine meal.

2. Add the tomato, lemon juice, scallion, garlic, sea salt, and 2 tablespoons of the flaxseed meal, and process until a thick paste has formed; add the quinoa and process until well combined.

3. Using a 1-inch ice-cream scoop, spoon the mixture onto a tray or cutting board.

4. Place the remaining 2 tablespoons flaxseed meal in a shallow bowl. Roll each falafel in the flaxseed and place on a dehydrator tray with the screen in place. Dehydrate at 118°F for 4 hours, or until the exterior crisps up.

*To sprout raw quinoa, cover the quinoa with water and soak for 8 to 12 hours at room temperature. (You'll see tiny tails on the grains.) Rinse and then use.

Note: The falafel can be stored in the refrigerator for up to 5 days. For an easy snack, roll the mixture inside a nori sheet with fresh cucumber and tahini!

MIXED-BERRY COCONUT JUBILEE

My son Dylan, like most kids, enjoys variety, even though he functions best with structure. Part of our routine is making this dish together. Dylan loves it because he can remember the steps. I love it because he's getting the nutrient boost of berries plus other ingredients that he might not taste otherwise.

....

1. In a blender combine the coconut flesh, coconut water, yacon syrup, hemp protein, probiotics, and sea salt. Blend well until rich and creamy. Refrigerate until ready to serve.

2. In a medium-size mixing bowl, lightly toss all the berries together.

3. In a parfait glass, layer the berries, the coconut mixture, and the berries again, topping with your choice of garnish.

Note: This recipe can be stored in the refrigerator for up to 5 days.

2 cups young Thai coconut flesh

½ cup coconut water

¼ cup yacon syrup or 3 drops liquid stevia

2 tablespoons hemp protein

1 tablespoon probiotics of choice (optional)

1 teaspoon sea salt

2 cups blueberries

2 cups hulled strawberry halves

2 cups raspberries

Diced avocado, mixed nuts, or seeds, for garnish

Makes 4 servings

For the crust:

2 cups walnuts or pecans

1 tablespoon cinnamon

1 teaspoon sea salt

½ cup raw agave nectar
  or raw honey

For the filling:

1 cup coconut water
  (regular water will also
  work)

1 cup raw cacao nibs

2 Hass avocados, peeled
  and pitted

1 tablespoon cinnamon

1 teaspoon sea salt

2 tablespoons
  supergreen powder
  (optional)

Makes
8 servings

CHOCOLATE CHEESECAKE

The most popular recipe in our household to date, Chocolate Cheesecake delivers more than 8 grams of protein per slice along with essential fatty acids, potassium, and vitamin E. Wow! Nutrients make this dessert a winner for Sunday dinner and the entire week.

1. To make the crust, in a food processor fitted with the S-blade, combine the nuts, cinnamon, and sea salt. Pulse until a fine meal is formed.

2. Add the agave through the feed tube and process until a dough ball has formed. (Be careful not to overprocess; with the nuts, the oil will separate.)

3. Line a 10-inch glass pie dish with the crust.

4. To make the filling, in a blender combine the coconut water, raw cacao nibs, avocado, cinnamon, sea salt, and supergreen powder. Blend until rich and creamy.

5. Pour the filling into the pie crust and smooth the top with an offset spatula or butter knife. (This mixture is also delicious as a pudding.)

6. Place the cheesecake into the freezer until firm, 1 to 2 hours. Remove, slice, and serve.

Note: The crust can be prepared in advance and stored in the freezer until use. The entire recipe can be stored in the freezer for up to 2 weeks. Thawing takes approximately 15 minutes.

For the crust:

1 cup raisins or dried
   figs, reconstituted

½ cup pecans

2 cups red quinoa,
   sprouted*

1 tablespoon cinnamon

1 teaspoon sea salt

For the filling:

½ cup raw almond butter

1 teaspoon cinnamon

¼ cup raw honey or
   2 drops liquid stevia

½ teaspoon sea salt

2 cups organic
   blueberries

Makes
8 tarts

ANCIENT GRAIN BLUEBERRY TARTS

Ancient grains are less common in the American pantry but are great health-enhancing additions. Quinoa, buckwheat, farro, and spelt are just a few samples you might find at your local health food store. Naturally gluten-free quinoa forms the high-protein base for these tarts. They're an ideal breakfast food or snack throughout the day.

1. To make the crust, in a food processor fitted with the S-blade, pulse the raisins until broken down but not runny.

2. Add the pecans, red quinoa, cinnamon, and sea salt, and process until a chunky dough has formed.

3. Press the crust into eight ½-inch-thick, 3-inch rounds on a baking sheet.

4. To make the filling, in a separate mixing bowl, combine the almond butter, cinnamon, raw honey, and sea salt, and whisk until well mixed.

5. Top each tart crust evenly with the mixture.

6. Finally, gently pulse the blueberries in the food processor or smash using a fork until the interiors are exposed. Top each tart evenly. Chill for 1 hour and enjoy.

*Although quinoa comes in three colors, the red version in this recipe offers a rich, full flavor. To sprout raw quinoa, cover the quinoa with water and soak for 8 to 12 hours at room temperature. (You'll see tiny tails on the grains.) Rinse and then use.

Note: The tarts can be stored in the refrigerator for up to 1 week.

HONEYDEW PIE POPS

These pie pops have found their way into this family section because their high-density nutrients are great for a developing body, especially the brain. But they're still a favorite of mine—so much so that I've been known to barter with my son for the remaining pop!

1. In a blender puree the honeydew, coconut butter, avocado, and raw honey until well combined. Add the fruit and toss gently by hand to combine.

2. Fill a standard-size pop mold with the mixture and place in the freezer for 4 to 6 hours. Enjoy!

Note: These pops can be stored in the freezer for up to 10 days.

1 large honeydew melon, seeded and flesh scooped out

½ cup coconut butter

1 Hass avocado

2 tablespoons raw honey or 2 drops liquid stevia

1 cup chopped fruit of choice (I love strawberries!)

Makes eight 6-ounce pops

A Final Note

Of course you have important reasons to make sure your children eat nutritiously. The plant-based recipes in this chapter can help you ensure your kids achieve and maintain their optimal weight and will satisfy the requirements for building strong bodies. The challenges are in keeping your menu balanced and interesting and partnering with a like-minded pediatrician who can monitor your child's nutritional progress. By doing both, you can positively impact a lifetime of eating. It's as important as making the changes I suggest in Chapter 12, "Food for a Healthy Soul."

CHAPTER 12

FOOD FOR A
HEALTHY SOUL

Did you ever think of food in terms of feeding your soul? It may sound like a trite feel-good notion, but you're the sum of your parts—mind, body, and spirit—and connecting positively with what you eat is important for overall optimal health.

Even the world's great religions recognize the power of food, whether feasting for celebration or fasting for personal growth. Yet you don't have to practice a specific religion to understand the connection between feeling physically satisfied and being emotionally satisfied. Whatever your spiritual touchstone, nourishing your inner being involves feeding your body with foods that support your soul. When you enjoy what you eat, you're more likely

to continue with the very choices that facilitate your overall well-being. You'll also experience the synergy that occurs when both your physical and your spiritual self are aligned. They work together for your greater good!

When the very act of eating made me sick, for instance, I wasn't living a life of creativity or higher purpose. My physical reactions affected my spirituality, imagination, and emotions. With the nutrient-rich diet I practice today, however, I feel in balance and a sense of oneness. By being aligned mentally, physically, and spiritually, I experience optimal health on all fronts. I'm energized and in harmony with the universe.

My experience reflects what science has repeatedly shown: Food can trigger immediate reactions within your body, in some cases stimulating a rush of brain chemicals, such as dopamine, serotonin, and endorphins. Along with changing your blood glucose, they can affect how you feel physically and emotionally. Cacao, or chocolate, for instance, binds with various chemicals in the brain to trigger or prolong euphoria. As such, it's long been regarded as the ultimate "feel-good food." (And a sweet staple in a raw-foods diet!)

The Soulful Solution

Healing with Raw Foods is full of what I call "soulful selections," plant-based choices that support your holistic being in multiple ways. Although the recipes you select will be unique to your taste buds and preferences, with each plant-based choice you make, you'll enjoy life-giving energy and nutrient content. For the very nature of *living* cuisine is the ability of each item to create a synergy between your physical body and your inner self.

Because living foods promote alkalinity, while delivering quality vitamins, minerals, antioxidants, essential fatty acids, and other nutrients to your cells, they can have a positive effect on your physical feelings. You experience fewer aches and pains and a reduced risk of disease. But you also feel better mentally, spiritually, and emotionally—a natural side effect of making positive dietary choices. You're not prone to the stresses and frustrations that come with toxins making your health chaotic. Instead, you can live joyfully.

And here's a bonus: Some studies suggest that our emotional response to a food transcends its actual chemical structure. In other words, just the color, smell, and texture can stimulate a positive response. Because living cuisine is replete with vibrant choices, it offers a rainbow of colorful options for soul-healthy results.

- *Vegetables:* Pumpkin, tomato, red bell pepper, dark leafy greens, herbs, beets
- *Fruits:* Coconut, tropical fruits, stone fruits (e.g., peaches), watermelon, pomegranate seeds, citrus fruits
- *Other:* Raw cacao, hemp seeds, quinoa, ginger root

By choosing "soulful selections"—foods that help you stay in physical and emotional alignment—you promote your own sense of peace, joy, and good health. You'll have balance and energy for reaching your highest dreams!

Advice from the Chef

To fortify the soul:

- Make your plate appealing. You eat with your eyes first, so add to the enjoyment by focusing on presentation for every meal.

- Garnish each dish with colorful toppers such as grated carrot; fresh herbs (cilantro, dill, or basil); or orange, lemon, or lime slices.

- Spice up dishes with cayenne, curry, ginger, or garlic. They stimulate not only your taste buds but your energy flow, too.

- Invigorate your spirit with tasty foods such as almond butter or other rich, creamy spreads. Raw cacao and colorful squashes are good, too.

- Eat soup! Tomato bisque is my favorite for the creamy texture. When served warm, it stimulates feel-good emotions in addition to supplying many nutrients.

Affirmations
for a Healthy Soul

How you feel has as much to do with how you think as it does with what you eat. Resolving, mentally and emotionally, to make healthy lifestyle changes is an important part of transitioning to living cuisine. When you're challenged, try these affirmations as "food for thought."

- "I am peaceful inside. My body and mind are working together to aid my total health and well-being."

- "I am grateful for my health and wellness."

SASSY STRAWBERRY SHAKE

Are you afraid to walk on the culinary wild side? This sassy smoothie is for you! It contains maca root, a natural stimulant, plus chia seeds for energy and strawberries to boost your metabolism.

1. Blend all the ingredients until a thick shake mixture has formed.

2. Add ice if you enjoy a frosty blend; otherwise, enjoy as is!

Note: This shake should be consumed on the same day it is blended.

½ banana

1 cup Almond Shortcut Milk (page 42)

½ cup hulled, sliced strawberries

⅓ cup young Thai coconut flesh or 1 tablespoon coconut butter

1 tablespoon maca root

1 tablespoon white chia seeds, soaked and drained

1 tablespoon raw cacao nibs (optional, makes a great crunch!)

Makes
1 serving

For the dehydrated salad mixture:

4 cups chopped broccoli

1 cup chopped green beans

½ cup finely sliced red onion

¼ cup extra-virgin olive oil

1 tablespoon raw agave nectar

1 tablespoon Italian Blend (page 23)

1 teaspoon sea salt

For the final salad:

1 cup finely diced squash

1 cup diced tomato

1 cup diced olives

1 cup finely chopped lacinato kale

Makes 4 servings

LIVE CHOPPED VEGGIE SALAD

By combining a spectrum of chopped vegetables in a single dish, this salad offers a balanced nutrient option for lunch or dinner. Because it can be refrigerated for up to a week, prepare it in advance. Then bring it out as an entrée or a side when you want a boost of vitamins, minerals, and enzymes.

1. To make the dehydrated salad mixture, in a mixing bowl combine the broccoli, green beans, red onion, olive oil, agave nectar, Italian Blend seasoning, and sea salt.

2. Line a dehydrator tray with a nonstick drying surface. Spread the salad mixture evenly over the tray.

3. Dehydrate at 118°F for 2 hours to soften the vegetables. If you don't have a dehydrator, let the vegetables sit for 2 hours to soften.

4. To make the final salad, in another mixing bowl, combine the squash, tomato, olives, and kale. Add the dehydrated salad mixture and toss to combine.

Note: This salad can be refrigerated for up to 5 days.

RAINBOW SPROUT SALAD

An intense supply of vitamins, minerals, proteins, and enzymes, sprouts are considered one of nature's most complete nutrient sources. They're also known as a very high-vibration food, meaning they emit energy that can lead to a strengthened immune system, increased vitality, and reduced stress.

1. To make the dressing, using an immersion blender, combine the olive oil, coconut aminos, garlic powder, chili powder, and stevia. Blend well.

2. To make the salad, in a large bowl, combine the sprouts, lettuce, green papaya, beets, sesame seeds, yam, and avocado; toss well.

3. Add the dressing and toss until coated. Enjoy immediately.

Note: The salad ingredients can be mixed earlier in the day and stored in the refrigerator until dressed for serving. Once combined with the dressing, the salad should be stored for no longer than 1 day.

For the dressing:

¼ cup extra-virgin olive oil

2 tablespoons coconut aminos

1 teaspoon garlic powder

1 teaspoon chili powder

1 drop liquid stevia

For the salad:

4 cups mixed sprouts

4 cups chopped romaine lettuce

1 cup shredded green papaya, jicama, or carrot

½ cup shredded beets

4 tablespoons black sesame seeds

½ cup diced steamed yam (optional, for transition)

½ Hass avocado, peeled, pitted, and diced

Makes 4 servings

1 large heirloom tomato
or 2 Roma tomatoes

2 sun-dried tomatoes

2 cups hot water*

4 fresh basil leaves or
⅓ cup chopped basil

1 tablespoon raw agave
nectar or raw honey

1 dried chipotle pepper,
seeded if desired

1 tablespoon dark chili
powder**

¼ cup extra-virgin
olive oil

Makes
1 entrée or
2 appetizer
servings

SPIRIT OF FIRE SOUP

Although igniting your passion is an inner journey, this basic soup will nourish your soul and light your fire while you're pursuing the path!

1. In a blender combine the tomatoes, hot water, basil, agave nectar, chipotle pepper, and chili powder. Blend well until a thick puree has formed.

2. While blending, add the olive oil to emulsify and thicken the soup.

*In living-cuisine prep, 100° to 110°F constitutes "hot"; 80° to 100°F constitutes "lukewarm." Temperatures can be measured easily with a standard candy thermometer.

**Dark chili powder provides a smokier taste than lighter versions, making it a better choice for this recipe.

Note: The soup can be stored in the refrigerator for up to 3 days.

7 CHAKRA TAPAS PLATTER

Little layered bites of love, these snacks are a great starter for your next dinner party or company meal. Laced with curry powder and stevia, these tapas deliver a sweet-savory taste. They're especially sweet when enjoyed with friends!

1. To make the sauce, in a blender combine the water, nuts, curry powder, coconut butter, garlic, and stevia until pureed.

2. To make the filling, in a medium-size mixing bowl, combine the red bell pepper, avocado, coconut, and basil. Add the sauce and toss until well coated.

3. To make the layers, slice the tomatoes into ½-inch-thick rounds and the yellow squash into ¼-inch-thick rounds.

4. For each appetizer, layer in the following order: 1 slice tomato, 2 tablespoons filling, 1 slice yellow squash, 2 tablespoons filling.

5. Top with the carrot curls and serve.

*Carrot curls are easily achieved by running a vegetable peeler the length of a carrot to shave thin pieces.

For the sauce:
½ cup water

¼ cup macadamia nuts

¼ cup curry powder

1 tablespoon coconut butter (optional)

1 clove garlic

1 drop liquid stevia

For the filling:
2 cups diced red bell pepper or tomato

2 cups diced avocado

1 cup young Thai coconut, cut into thin strips

1 cup chopped basil

For the layers:
2 Roma or heirloom tomatoes

1 yellow crookneck squash

1 cup carrot curls*

Makes
4 appetizer
servings

For the crust:

2 cups raw coconut flour

1 tablespoon raw coconut butter

3 drops liquid stevia, ¼ cup yacon syrup, or ½ cup raw apple juice

For the filling:

2 cups young Thai coconut flesh

¼ cup lemon juice

1 teaspoon sea salt

3 drops liquid stevia or ¼ cup yacon syrup

2 cups raspberries

½ cup shredded coconut

¼ cup lemon zest

Makes 6 servings

RAZZAMATAZZ PIE

Raspberries, lemons, and coconut come together in this flavorful concoction that's simple to make and fun to eat. Although great as a dessert, it's also a refreshing option for starting the day.

1. To make the crust, in a food processor fitted with the S-blade, combine the coconut flour, coconut butter, and stevia. Pulse until a crust-like dough has formed.

2. Press the crust into a 10-inch glass pie plate.

3. To make the filling, in a blender combine the coconut flesh, lemon juice, sea salt, and stevia. Blend.

4. Spread the filling atop the crust, smoothing with an offset spatula or butter knife.

5. Top the filling with the raspberries, then sprinkle with the coconut and lemon zest.

6. Refrigerate and enjoy throughout the entire week.

Note: The pie can be stored in the refrigerator for up to 5 days.

CACAO HAZELNUT FUDGE

With this candy sensation, you don't need traditional chocolate to satisfy your sweet tooth. Cacao Hazelnut Fudge combines the nutrient benefits of nuts and protein powder with the antioxidant properties of cacao powder and coconut butter. Add cayenne pepper for an even more invigorating snack!

1. In a blender combine the cacao powder, coconut nectar, coconut butter, protein supplement, cinnamon, cayenne pepper, sea salt, and nutmeg until rich and creamy.

2. In a medium-size mixing bowl, toss the hazelnut pieces with the cacao mixture.

3. Pour the mixture onto a flat tray or an 8 × 8-inch glass dish.

4. Freeze the mixture for about 8 hours, then cut into 16 pieces and enjoy.

Note: This recipe can be stored in the freezer indefinitely.

1 cup raw cacao powder

½ cup coconut nectar or yacon syrup

¼ cup coconut butter or cacao butter

2 tablespoons Warrior Food or other plant-based protein supplement

1 tablespoon cinnamon

1 teaspoon cayenne pepper (optional)

1 teaspoon sea salt

¼ teaspoon nutmeg

2 cups hazelnut pieces

Makes sixteen 2 × 2-inch pieces

⅔ cup raw agave nectar

⅓ cup coconut butter or fresh coconut flesh

¼ teaspoon sea salt or Himalayan salt

2 drops mint essential oil (optional)

2 cups raw cacao powder

Makes eight 2-inch hearts

CHOCOLATE MINI HEARTS

The cacao and other ingredients packaged in this great candy substitute offer a healthy dose of magnesium and brain-stimulating amino acids. Chocolate Mini Hearts are a chocolate lover's best friend. They're a guilt-free way to indulge at any time of the day!

1. In a blender combine the agave nectar, coconut butter, sea salt, and mint essential oil. Blend until well combined.

2. Add the cacao and blend until a frosting-like mixture has formed.

3. Spread the mixture into 8 ungreased heart molds. Freeze for at least 6 hours.

4. Remove from the freezer 15 minutes before serving; unmold and top with a fresh rose petal for a fun (but not edible!) presentation.

Note: These can be stored in the freezer indefinitely.

CHOCOLATE FROSTING DROPS

Yum! Chocolate Frosting Drops are just one use for this easy-to-prepare mixture that can also serve as a cake or dessert topper or as a layer in a scrumptious parfait cup. As a feel-good recipe, it's sure to stimulate your soul!

....

1. In a blender combine all the ingredients and blend for 2 minutes, or until thick.

2. Pour the mixture into a piping bag fitted with the tip of your choice. Place in the freezer for 30 minutes to firm up.

3. Remove the piping bag from the freezer. Line a tray with a nonstick sheet and squeeze out perfectly fluffy cacao frosting shots in the shape and size of your choice.

4. Allow the shots to become firm before serving. Serve with love and sprinkle with extra spices like cinnamon for added flair.

*Irish moss is an edible seaweed, so named because it grows along the shoreline of Ireland as well as the rocky Atlantic seaboard.

Note: These drops can be stored in the refrigerator for up to 2 weeks.

2 cups raw cacao powder

2 cups warm water

½ cup raw agave nectar

2 tablespoons Irish moss*

Pinch of sea salt

Makes about 12 drops

½ cup creamed raw honey

¼ cup maca powder

1 teaspoon sea salt

4 cups almond flour (may use meal if flour is unavailable)

6 tablespoons white cacao

Makes
12 cookies

WHITE CACAO COOKIES

White chocolate has been a favorite among my friends, even though the sad truth is that most white chocolate isn't chocolate at all! This recipe uses the true stuff—raw white chocolate extracted from the fat solids of cacao. You can typically find it online.

1. In a food processor fitted with the S-blade, process the raw honey, maca, and sea salt until well combined.

2. Add the almond flour and 4 tablespoons of the white cacao. Process lightly so the cookie dough still has body and the white cacao is somewhat chunky.

3. Scoop into twelve 2-inch round cookies and place on a dehydrator tray lined with a nonstick drying sheet. (Or place in a glass baking dish.)

4. Finely chop the remaining 2 tablespoons of white cacao and sprinkle over the tops of the cookies.

5. Dehydrate the cookies for 2 hours at 118°F, or until dry to the touch, or simply enjoy in their raw state.

Note: These cookies can be stored in the refrigerator for up to 1 week.

A Final Note

Living cuisine is more than a dietary plan of nutrient-rich foods selected to sustain your physical well-being. It's an acknowledgment that you're the sum total of all your parts, with mind, body, and spirit working synergistically for your greater good. As such, you need to nourish your soul just like you're nourishing your body. Plant-based ingredients provide that connection in multiple ways, starting with a cache of nutrients that keep you energized, positive, and in tip-top shape. By first supporting you physically, these recipes are truly food for a healthy soul.

AFTERWORD

Progress Every Day

I hope that you find *Healing with Raw Foods* a helpful road map for a healthier life. Until now, you may not have thought of food as a force for healing. As a culture, we too often wait for a health crisis to spur us to modify our diets. We forget that what we eat each day has enormous implications on how well our bodies function and ward off disease. We don't think of its commanding role in the prevention of disease.

This cookbook was written to refocus your attention, to inspire you in making healthier choices step by step, day by day, one bite at a time. My goal with each recipe is to encourage you to explore your options, experiment with new ingredients, and expand your raw-food knowledge. I'm confident that once you learn how a plant-based diet can promote wellness, you'll want to live life the living-foods way. By incorporating the "good stuff" every day, you'll be accomplishing your health goals in a meaningful way.

Ten Steps to Healthy Eating

Because the path to longevity depends in large part on choices that support and revitalize, rather than degrade or overwork, your body, you should be working every day to eliminate toxins and toxic foods. By replacing them with supernutritive ingredients, you're cleansing your systems and oxygenating your cells.

Keep in mind that a diet comprising 70 to 80 percent living foods can jump-start good health throughout your body by infusing each part with abundant vitamins, minerals, enzymes, amino acids, and other nutrients. Although *Healing with Raw Foods* contains many recipes, you can make a preemptive, preventive strike for your future well-being by changing your eating habits with just one food at a time! Remodeling your diet can begin with these ten simple steps.

1. **Start right.** Begin each day with a balanced raw-foods meal. Although many people find fresh fruits a great way to break the fast, I encourage rounding out the first meal of the day with healthy fats to get both brain and body going. Fruit bowls with avocado, superfood smoothies, and coconut yogurt or other parfaits are a good breakfast fit.

2. **Embrace a salad and greens.** Try veggies as a side to your entrée favorite, and you may eventually want to make it a main dish. A salad is a ready way of providing your body with necessary fiber, vitamins, and minerals. If you make a salad a meal, make sure you cover your protein bases by adding quinoa, walnuts, or other nutrient-rich foods to balance the dish. Dark leafy greens provide a great foundation for a healthy diet because they contain multiple nutrients, so incorporate at least a half cup at every meal.

3. **Add whole foods and superfoods.** Yams and other whole or unprocessed vegetables are a good choice for any daily meal. Even if they're steamed, baked, or parboiled, they don't contain additives or fillers, which makes them a great transitional item for your diet. You can incorporate enzymes and other nutrients into any meal by topping with a raw-food sauce. In terms of superfoods, adding a tablespoon of hemp seeds and goji berries to any dish, even tea, can increase the vitamins, minerals, and enzymes, which quickly bolster your nutrient intake. Remember, great health is cumulative. The more *living* the ingredients, the better you'll feel!

4. **Trade in the milk carton.** By making your own almond, hemp, or other nut milk, you're supplying your body with antioxidants plus some fat and protein. You're also protecting yourself from the saturated fat and cholesterol in cow's milk and the additives in store-bought almond-milk brands.

5. **Simplify!** Eating raw foods can be as simple as placing raw almond butter on fresh apple slices for a snack. I was so passionate about the possibilities when I started with this eating plan that I made apples with tahini crème and raw honey my go-to food for months. I felt fantastic!

6. **Plan a food prep day.** Choose one day of the week to prepare fresh basics. If you're pressed for time, focus on one salad dressing, one snack (Moxie Bars, page 75, are great), and a raw sauce, such as Tahini Crème (page 177). If you're flush with time, add other spreads, crackers, and breads to your to-do list. By making these items early, you're ready in a pinch to match them with last-minute salads, sandwiches, and other fresh dishes.

7. **Shop outside the box.** A raw-foods diet encourages you to go beyond a traditional grocery store to your local farmers' market, co-op, health store, Asian market, or online resource. By visiting these alternative retailers regularly, you'll continually expand your living- and organic food choices. You'll be surprised at the new items you spot each time you explore. My shopping trips are still fun adventures, even after a decade devoted to the living-cuisine lifestyle.

8. **Create your own drink.** A daily smoothie of fresh, living ingredients guarantees that the foods you're receiving are 100 percent functional for your body. A meal-in-a-cup delivers a variety of essential nutrients. Experiment by sampling the recipes in this book or just combining raw choices you enjoy into a potion you can drink every day or several times a week. Change the content as your health merits. And don't forget to share with your friends. A smoothie is a quick way of introducing this eating style to others.

9. **Stay hydrated.** Besides aiding in digestion and flushing out toxins, water is essential in other functions, such as carrying nutrition to your cells. Lack of water can lead to dehydration, which can drain your energy and make you think you're hungry when you're not. How much water do you need? Although the Institute of Medicine suggests roughly 13 cups a day of liquid for men and 9 cups a day for women, an easy rule of thumb is "8 by 8": Drink 8 ounces of liquid eight times a day.

10. **Keep adding favorites.** The more good stuff you introduce into your diet, the less room you'll have for foods that don't serve your higher purpose. So begin each day and shopping experience by asking yourself, "What can I add that will benefit my health?" Keep referring back to your recent experiences with new food items to

identify new favorites. It may be helpful to keep a food journal for this very reason. Remember also that health is cumulative. Every decision you make can add up to positive results.

A Final Note

The beauty of living cuisine is that it's about more than just replacing dietary toxins with healthy food choices. It's also about creating a holistic life that looks and feels different than anything you've felt in the past. It's about being positive and moving forward! That means eliminating the other poisons—negative emotions, addictive substances, and environmental pollutants—in your orbit so you can experience the full benefits of a life in balance. If healthy recipes and live ingredients are the means of healing your physical being, then daily affirmations, journaling, exercise, visualizations, inner reflections, and acts of simple gratitude are the means of healing your mind and spirit, too. By bringing these forces together, you're able to embrace the day with unbridled energy, confidence, and peace. It's my hope that *Healing with Raw Foods* will help you start and complete that journey.

APPENDIX I

Cook Like a Chef: A Guide to Quality Utensils

Just as moving into a new home can bring out your inner designer, setting up a living-cuisine kitchen can spark your inner chef. By investing in the kind of utensils and appliances that cooking pros rely on every day, you can ease the stress of preparation even in your own kitchen. If your budget allows only two items initially, however, I suggest a high-powered blender and mandoline. By giving you mixing and slicing efficiency, they'll increase your culinary confidence, function, and fun. And here's the bonus: Like all my favorite kitchen things, they're readily available in stores and online. You don't need to cast your net wide for appliances or utensils that work.

Appliances

Blenders

A blender is a must-have in a living-cuisine kitchen. My preference is a high-powered model because it's perfect not only for creating salad dressings and other creamy sauces but also for breaking down the fibrous cell walls of whole fruits and vegetables and pulverizing nuts and seeds. How so? A 1,000- to 1,560-watt motor offers extra flexibility for many cooking tasks—from whipping and pureeing to grinding and chopping—without straining or overheating. Of course, you can perform many of my recipe tasks with a basic blender. A 500- to 750-watt motor still chops and blends efficiently. But if you're cooking with a slower model, try these tips: Blend all liquids and soft vegetables first before adding heavier ingredients, or divide the recipe into smaller batches and blend separately before combining in a bowl later.

Features/Brands: I recommend brands that both professional and home chefs find useful because they're tough and deliver over time. Vitamix and Dynablend blenders by Tribestlife top my list. If you're looking for a traditional kitchen model, however, you'll find a great selection in retail outlets.

Dehydrators

You may not be familiar with this appliance yet, but you'll soon discover the value of a dehydrator. Because it circulates warm air slowly around food, such as fruits and vegetables, to remove moisture, it doesn't "bake" out the essential nutrients as with traditional cooking. A dehydrator can give you great versatility, not to mention savings, because you're able to create flavorful dehydrated snacks and separates. It's wonderful for "baking" allergen-free breads, crackers, and wraps to replace commercial pastries that contain potentially harmful wheat, corn, and other grains. One tip, however, about the recipes in this book: Although many call for a dehydrator, some may utilize alternative preparations, which you'll find in the notes.

Features/Brands: The Sedona nine-tray dehydrator (by Tribestlife) is the best such appliance on the market for raw-food preparation. It features duel temperature controls and silicone trays free of bisphenol-A (BPA), a chemical linked to a wide variety of health issues. Because you'll also need to purchase either parchment paper or nonstick drying sheets, make sure they're also made of BPA-free silicone. The ones we feature at www.118degrees.com and those available through www.Tribest.com are easy to clean and reusable. Thinner Teflex sheets are available through many online raw-foods suppliers.

Food Processors

A food processor is a time-saver, especially for mixing thick-bodied and thick-textured recipes such as chutneys, heavy spreads, nut butters, and salsas, plus breads, dessert crusts, cookies, crackers, and other doughs. It slices and dices faster than you likely can move a knife over a cutting board, saving prep time.

Features/Brands: The most important features of a food processor are the S-shaped blade and a 10- to 12-cup bowl. Most models include other discs for kneading, grating, and pureeing, but you need the basic S-blade for everyday raw-food preparation. Cuisinart and Waring food processors meet my specifications because they're simple to use and easily adapted to many recipes.

Juicers

A juicer is just what the name implies: It allows you to create fresh juices from fruits and vegetables for a quick pick-me-up. Although juicing can be messy, with a good juicer, you can limit the process to every few days and still enjoy the healthy benefits daily. In addition, the leftover pulp can be integrated into bread and cracker recipes as fiber. Depending on your needs, you'll want to use one of the following two models:

- *Masticating (twin-gear) juicer.* Like your teeth, the stainless-steel twin gears of a masticating juicer chew, grind, or knead fruits and vegetables into pulp, squishing out liquid. By operating at a relatively slow speed, a twin-gear juicer creates limited heat and friction, which is key in maintaining enzyme and overall nutrient quality while extracting more juice than other machines.

- *Centrifugal juicer.* As the term *centrifugal* implies, this juicer spins liquid outward from the center collection bin as fruits or vegetables are ground into pulp. The biggest plus is its speed. Because the motor operates at a very high velocity, it processes juice very, very quickly. Also, the feeding chute is large, so whole fruit can be juiced at once. If you're eager to enjoy juice right away, a centrifugal model definitely fits the bill.

Features/Brands: If you're purchasing a twin-gear or masticating juicer, I recommend either the Champion or Green Star brand. Both can be an investment, but they do the job beautifully. If you're not quite ready to spend large, however, I suggest a centrifugal model. Although there are many brands on the market, my choice is a Breville because it works well for the price. Whatever your target, juicers are readily available through cooking stores and other retail outlets.

Utensils

Bowls/Storage Containers

Glass bowls and storage containers are the safest and most reliable way to serve and store your culinary creations. In retooling your kitchen for living-food cuisine, you'll want to recycle any plastic glasses, bowls, or other containers, because many of them contain harmful BPA. Not only is BPA found in many plastic products, but it's also known to leach into foods stored in or served from them. So for the sake of your health, think glass.

Features/Brands: Fortunately, in today's culinary marketplace, you'll find many, many acceptable glass and Pyrex substitutes for plastic bowls, containers, serving pieces, and measuring cups. They're plentiful online and through every store that sells kitchen items. Start with at least one small bowl for whisking sauces, one medium-size bowl for mixing salads, and one large bowl for mixing big batches.

Stoneware or Ceramic-Coated Kettles and Frying Pans

Because recipes in this book sometimes involve light blanching and steaming, you need to invest in cookware that won't interfere with any nutritional value. I recommend stoneware kettles and frying pans because they're created from clay and other quality materials fired at extremely high temperatures. They won't negate the nutritious benefits of an organic dish by leaching toxins. Other options include cast-iron or stainless-steel items fired with an enamel or a porcelain coating. It seals the underlying metal from any potential leaching.

Features/Brands: There are many suitable stoneware cookware brands on the market. As for enamel-coated cookware, I prefer Le Creuset's extensive line of stainless-steel and cast-iron products. Whatever you buy, make sure that the cooking surface isn't covered with Teflon or another synthetic nonstick coating. You want your food to touch only stoneware or a porcelain coating.

Mandoline

Mandoline slicers are great options for creating squash pasta, lasagna, marinated vegetables, and other raw-food dishes. These stand-alone devices make cutting uniform slices simple and fast. Mandolines work by sliding the fruit or vegetable over a razor-sharp blade that can be adjusted from paper-thin to 1-inch widths. Most mandolines come with julienne-cut and other blade options for varying widths and shapes.

Features/Brands: Mandolines are available at all prices and retail outlets, under many brand names. I recommend either the Choisons V-Slicer (by Tribestlife), which stands sturdily upright on the kitchen counter, or the OXO Good Grips Mandoline. It has a rotating blade attachment that can be very useful. Both models can be purchased with ceramic blades, which not only glide through the food effortlessly but also won't taint it in the process.

Santoku Knife

A Japanese invention, the Santoku knife is ideally suited for transitioning to a plant-based diet because it's sharp and easy to manipulate. Its characteristic features include a shorter, thinner, straighter blade and less-pointed tip than an American chef's knife. Small notches or scallops along the edge enable air to enter between the blade and the fruit or vegetable, which allows for quicker chopping action and a cleaner, safer cut.

Brands/Features: There are many brands and styles of Santoku knives available both online and through your favorite kitchen store. I recommend a ceramic blade because it helps prevent oxidation of fruits and vegetables. It also holds its sharpness longer than a stainless-steel blade. The Santoku knives I find very easy to use are from Choisons and Global. Whatever you purchase, look for a knife with a 6- to 8-inch blade.

Wooden Cutting Boards and Bowls

Natural wooden cutting boards are important for hands-on use in creating the recipes in this book. For a clean and healthy workplace, I recommend products made of "sustainable" or renewable woods such as bamboo, acacia, or olive, which also aren't coated with a sealant. Wooden cutting boards can be easily cleaned with hydrogen peroxide to keep them free of bacteria and then coated with a little fresh oil to maintain the wood. These natural materials won't affect your food in any inorganic way.

Features/Brands: Sustainable-wood cutting boards and bowls are readily available in most kitchen and other retail stores.

APPENDIX II

RAW-FOOD PYRAMID

Medicinal Foods
& Superfoods

**High Nutrient Value
Small Portions**

Jenny's Favorites: Dulse,
Hemp Seeds, Raw Cacao,
Chia Seeds, Maca Root

Herbs, Microgreens
& Wheat Grass Juice

Nuts & Seeds
Flax/Hemp

**Proteins, Amino Acids
Eat Moderately**

Jenny's Favorites: Tahini,
Pumpkin Seeds, Avocado,
Coconut, Buckwheat

Sprouts
Legumes

Fruits
Vegetables

**Foundation Foods
Eat Generously**

Jenny's Favorites:
Kale, Spinach, Chard,
Nappa Cabbage,
Mixed Baby Greens

Leafy Greens

APPENDIX III

Biographies

While working on this manuscript, I had the great honor to interview and consult with doctors who are pioneering the field of integrative medicine in their own areas of expertise. These experts have committed to partnering with their clients to help them heal naturally whenever possible. They have encouraged and empowered many on their paths to total wellness and bring a wealth of knowledge to this work through their ongoing research and clinical practices. The insights they have shared with me are woven throughout this book to best assist you in putting their practical knowledge to work in specified areas of healing.

These doctors took their time between patients and educating their peers, often in the wee hours of the morning, because of their passionate purpose to help get this information out to empower those who can use it to move their health forward in a positive direction. We have profiled these dedicated professionals so you may further connect to their work and take the next steps to finding your own perfect health. Personally, I'd like to add that I have searched the globe over for experts to contribute in these fields, and I can say with certainty that these doctors have stood out head and shoulders above the rest through their work and the results they have achieved; their time was invaluable to the making of this book, and through them my own health has catapulted. To hear the full interviews, please visit www.jennyross livingfoods.com.

Dr. Daniel Amen

Daniel G. Amen, M.D., is medical director of the Amen Clinics, Inc., a Costa Mesa, California–based network of treatment facilities for a wide range of addictive, emotional, and behavioral issues. A pioneering advocate of brain imaging and natural, brain-oriented approaches, Dr. Amen is a Distinguished Fellow of the American Psychiatric Association; an assistant clinical professor of psychiatry and human behavior at the University of California, Irvine School of Medicine; and the author of numerous peer-reviewed articles and books, including three *New York Times* bestsellers. Amen has also produced and starred in five public television programs about the brain.

Dr. Gabriel Cousens

Gabriel Cousens, M.D., M.D.(H), and D.D., is a leading live-food and spiritual nutrition expert. The founding director of the Tree of Life Rejuvenation Center, he's a best-selling author of numerous books, including *There Is a Cure for Diabetes*. Besides earning a medical degree from Columbia University Medical School with residency training in psychiatry, Dr. Cousens also holds divinity and holistic medical degrees. He's a recognized homeopath, acupuncturist, and Diplomate practitioner of Ayurveda, the Hindu traditional medicine. Dr. Cousens's alternative-health endeavors have earned him various recognitions, including that of the "fasting guru" and "detoxification expert" by the *New York Times*.

Dr. Caldwell Esselstyn

A world-renowned endocrine and breast disease surgeon, Caldwell B. Esselstyn, Jr., M.D., is also a prolific researcher whose work has solidified the link between diet and disease. His 20-year groundbreaking nutritional study is featured in *Forks Over Knives*, a documentary exploring how degenerative diseases can be controlled or even reversed with a whole-foods diet. Dr. Esselstyn is a consultant staff physician with the Cleveland Clinic, where he's been affiliated since 1968. The author of more than 150 scientific publications, he's the recipient of many honors, including the first Benjamin Spock Award for Compassion in Medicine.

Dr. Robert Morse

A board-certified and accredited naturopathic physician, Robert S. Morse, N.D., D.Sc., I.D., M.H., is also trained as a biochemist and master herbalist. A prolific author and lecturer, Dr. Morse has taught countless physicians and other health-care professionals about the benefits of detoxification and cellular regeneration and their role in healing. He has also treated thousands of people with varied conditions using the principles and steps now recorded in *The Detox Miracle Sourcebook*. Certified by the American Naturopathic Medical Certification and Accreditation Board, Dr. Morse is the founder of God's Herbs Botanical Company in Port Charlotte, Florida.

Dr. Michael Shannon

Michael W. Shannon began practicing in California's Saddleback Valley in 1973, originally in Mission Viejo, and since 1996 has been in the Laguna Hills office of Sea View Pediatrics. A graduate of Northwestern University Medical School, with residency training at Children's Hospital Los Angeles, Dr. Shannon has a special interest in infant and toddler growth and development as well as first-child parenting. "My basic philosophy about children," he says, "is that we must listen to what they tell us from their first sound and facilitate their development of *self*, beginning at birth."

METRIC CONVERSION CHART

The recipes in this book use the standard United States method for measuring liquid and dry or solid ingredients (teaspoons, tablespoons, and cups). The following charts are provided to help cooks outside the U.S. successfully use these recipes. All equivalents are approximate.

Standard Cup	Fine Powder (e.g., flour)	Grain (e.g., rice)	Granular (e.g., sugar)	Liquid Solids (e.g., butter)	Liquid (e.g., milk)
1	140 g	150 g	190 g	200 g	240 ml
¾	105 g	113 g	143 g	150 g	180 ml
⅔	93 g	100 g	125 g	133 g	160 ml
½	70 g	75 g	95 g	100 g	120 ml
⅓	47 g	50 g	63 g	67 g	80 ml
¼	35 g	38 g	48 g	50 g	60 ml
⅛	18 g	19 g	24 g	25 g	30 ml

Useful Equivalents for Liquid Ingredients by Volume				
¼ tsp				1 ml
½ tsp				2 ml
1 tsp				5 ml
3 tsp	1 tbsp		½ fl oz	15 ml
	2 tbsp	⅛ cup	1 fl oz	30 ml
	4 tbsp	¼ cup	2 fl oz	60 ml
	5⅓ tbsp	⅓ cup	3 fl oz	80 ml
	8 tbsp	½ cup	4 fl oz	120 ml
	10⅔ tbsp	⅔ cup	5 fl oz	160 ml
	12 tbsp	¾ cup	6 fl oz	180 ml
	16 tbsp	1 cup	8 fl oz	240 ml
	1 pt	2 cups	16 fl oz	480 ml
	1 qt	4 cups	32 fl oz	960 ml
			33 fl oz	1000 ml	1 l

Useful Equivalents for Dry Ingredients by Weight

(To convert ounces to grams, multiply the number of ounces by 30.)

1 oz	1/16 lb	30 g
4 oz	1/4 lb	120 g
8 oz	1/2 lb	240 g
12 oz	3/4 lb	360 g
16 oz	1 lb	480 g

Useful Equivalents for Cooking/Oven Temperatures

Process	Fahrenheit	Celsius	Gas Mark
Freeze Water	32° F	0° C	
Room Temperature	68° F	20° C	
Boil Water	212° F	100° C	
Bake	325° F	160° C	3
	350° F	180° C	4
	375° F	190° C	5
	400° F	200° C	6
	425° F	220° C	7
	450° F	230° C	8
Broil			Grill

Useful Equivalents for Length

(To convert inches to centimeters, multiply the number of inches by 2.5.)

1 in			2.5 cm	
6 in	1/2 ft		15 cm	
12 in	1 ft		30 cm	
36 in	3 ft	1 yd	90 cm	
40 in			100 cm	1 m

RECIPE INDEX

ABOUT THE AUTHOR

Jenny Ross, the owner and executive chef of the living-foods restaurant chain 118 Degrees, in Orange County, California, has been a pioneering spirit of the raw-foods movement since 2000, beginning with her first Los Angeles café. Her unique creations as a chef have captivated customers nationwide, and her product line is available in health food stores throughout the country.

Jenny works with clients of all backgrounds, motivating them toward more vibrant health while teaching them about the healing power of living foods. Her award-winning cuisine has drawn a celebrity clientele to her restaurant and has been a positive catalyst for changing many lives. She is a mind-body practitioner with a degree in holistic nutrition. Using food as a healing force is the basis of her work, her business, and her life.

Websites: www.jennyrosslivingfoods.com; www.118degrees.com; www.lemon dropjuice.com

Hay House Titles of Related Interest

YOU CAN HEAL YOUR LIFE, *the movie*, starring Louise Hay & Friends
(available as a 1-DVD program and an expanded 2-DVD set)
Watch the trailer at: www.LouiseHayMovie.com

THE SHIFT, *the movie*, starring Dr. Wayne W. Dyer
(available as a 1-DVD program and an expanded 2-DVD set)
Watch the trailer at: www.DyerMovie.com

ANGEL DETOX: *Taking Your Life to a Higher Level Through Releasing Emotional, Physical, and Energetic Toxins,* by Doreen Virtue and Robert Reeves, N.D.

THE BODY ECOLOGY GUIDE TO GROWING YOUNGER: *Anti-Aging Wisdom for Every Generation,* by Donna Gates, with Lyndi Schrecengost

CRAZY SEXY KITCHEN: *150 Plant-Empowered Recipes to Ignite a Mouthwatering Revolution,* by Kris Carr, with Chef Chris Sarno

CULTURED FOOD FOR LIFE: *How to Make and Serve Delicious Probiotic Foods for Better Health and Wellness,* by Donna Schwenk

THE LOONEYSPOONS COLLECTION: *Good Food, Good Health, Good Fun!,* by Janet and Greta Podleski

MEALS THAT HEAL INFLAMMATION: *Embrace Healthy Living and Eliminate Pain, One Meal at a Time,* by Julie Daniluk, R.H.N.

MINDFUL EATING, by Miraval

THE PLANT PLUS DIET SOLUTION: *Personalized Nutrition for Life,* by Joan Borysenko, Ph.D.

All of the above are available at your local bookstore,
or may be ordered by contacting Hay House (see next page).

We hope you enjoyed this Hay House book. If you'd like
to receive our online catalog featuring additional information
on Hay House books and products, or if you'd like to find
out more about the Hay Foundation, please contact:

Hay House, Inc., P.O. Box 5100, Carlsbad, CA 92018-5100
(760) 431-7695 or (800) 654-5126
(760) 431-6948 (fax) or (800) 650-5115 (fax)
www.hayhouse.com® • www.hayfoundation.org

Published and distributed in Australia by: Hay House Australia Pty. Ltd.,
18/36 Ralph St., Alexandria NSW 2015 • *Phone: 612-9669-4299*
Fax: 612-9669-4144 • www.hayhouse.com.au

Published and distributed in the United Kingdom by: Hay House UK, Ltd.,
Astley House, 33 Notting Hill Gate, London W11 3JQ • *Phone: 44-20-3675-2450*
Fax: 44-20-3675-2451 • www.hayhouse.co.uk

Published and distributed in the Republic of South Africa by: Hay House SA (Pty), Ltd., P.O.
Box 990, Witkoppen 2068 • *Phone/Fax: 27-11-467-8904* • www.hayhouse.co.za

Published in India by: Hay House Publishers India, Muskaan Complex,
Plot No. 3, B-2, Vasant Kunj, New Delhi 110 070 • *Phone: 91-11-4176-1620*
Fax: 91-11-4176-1630 • www.hayhouse.co.in

Distributed in Canada by: Raincoast Books, 2440 Viking Way, Richmond, B.C.
V6V 1N2 • *Phone: 1-800-663-5714* • *Fax: 1-800-565-3770* • www.raincoast.com

Take Your Soul on a Vacation

Visit www.HealYourLife.com® to regroup, recharge,
and reconnect with your own magnificence.
Featuring blogs, mind-body-spirit news, and life-changing
wisdom from Louise Hay and friends.

Visit www.HealYourLife.com today!

Free e-newsletters from Hay House, the Ultimate Resource for Inspiration

Be the first to know about Hay House's dollar deals, free downloads, special offers, affirmation cards, giveaways, contests, and more!

 Get exclusive excerpts from our latest releases and videos from *Hay House Present Moments*.

 Enjoy uplifting personal stories, how-to articles, and healing advice, along with videos and empowering quotes, within *Heal Your Life*.

 Have an inspirational story to tell and a passion for writing? Sharpen your writing skills with insider tips from *Your Writing Life*.

Sign Up Now!

Get inspired, educate yourself, get a complimentary gift, and share the wisdom!

http://www.hayhouse.com/newsletters.php

Visit www.hayhouse.com to sign up today!

 HAY HOUSE

 HAYHOUSE RADIO
radio for your soul®

HealYourLife.com